RUGBY LEA

MEMORIES

Including 'Rugby League in the 'Forties'

RUGBY LEAGUE JOURNAL

PUBLISHING

P.O. Box 22, Egremont, Cumbria, CA23 3WA
E-Mail: rugbyleague.journal@sky.com   Telephone: 01946 811005
www.rugbyleaguejournal.com

RUGBY LEAGUE MEMORIES

First published in Great Britain in 2015
ISBN 978-0-9932931-0-8

This is the sixth volume published in the 'Rugby League Journal History Series'.

Written and designed by Harry Edgar
Sales and marketing by Ruth Edgar
Printed by the Firpress Group Limited

Front cover main picture:
Alan Hardisty for Castleford in 1969.
Inset pictures:
Alex Murphy, Tom Van Vollenhoven and Neil Fox.
Frontispiece page picture:
Neil Fox for Wakefield Trinity in 1962.

The publisher wishes to thank old friends Eddie Whitham and Andrew Varley for their pictures, and all the photographers of the past who created the many wonderful images which illustrate this book. Their work has stood the test of time.

This book is dedicated to the memory of Joseph H. Edgar (1923 - 1986)

Your can order further copies of this book by sending a cheque for £14.95 (including £2.00 p&p) - payable to 'Rugby League Journal' - to: Rugby League Journal, P.O.Box 22, Egremont, Cumbria, CA23 3WA. You can also order our quarterly magazine 'Rugby League Journal' - price £4.50 for a single issue or £18 for annual subscription (four issues) including postage. Also available from our website: www.rugbyleaguejournal.com

Contents

Rugby League in the 'Forties

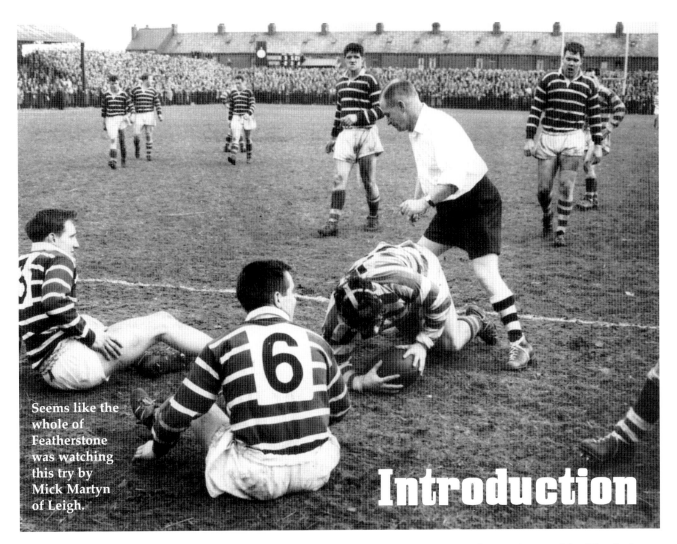

Seems like the whole of Featherstone was watching this try by Mick Martyn of Leigh.

Introduction

THIS is the sixth volume to be published in our 'Rugby League Journal History Series' and, as you will see, it actually presents two different books inside one cover.

We have already published volumes covering the decades of the 1950s, '60s, '70s and '80s, and the second half of this book featuring the 1940s follows a similar style to those previous volumes, recording the major finals, international matches and tours. The era of the immediate post-war years is one of the most vibrant and exciting in the whole history of Rugby League, and I certainly would have had no problems in filling a full volume just on the 1940s. Alas, commercial pressures make that unfeasible, but a small number of 'Rugby League Journal' readers asked me to do 'the 'Forties' and so, as a favour to them, here's the best I could afford.

Those post-war years were a wonderful time for international Rugby League, with record breaking tours and a vibrant European Championship. Those are high among the things I miss most in the modern game. And those years in the second half of the 1940s have always held a special fascination for me because they were the most positive and exciting in the two areas of the game I have the closest affinity to - in Cumberland and in France.

Before you get to the section on 'the 'Forties' you can enjoy a selection of 'Rugby League Memories' which takes us on a journey of nostalgia to many places so many readers will remember visiting themselves - to the old grounds, and seeing the teams and players, of the past. All this is based on a large and varied selection of wonderful old photographs which bring those memories to life.

To mark the personal milestone of reaching my 40th year of publishing Rugby League magazines, I thought it would be enjoyable to drop in a few of my own memories of growing up with the game. So in the pages that follow, you will pick up a few snippets about the first game I saw, the first Wembley Final, the first Kangaroo touring team, and a few encounters with some of the game's best known players and personalities.

I hope this book will encourage readers to enjoy their own similar memories and I am sure many, like me, were first introduced to the game by their father. In these reminisces you will see numerous references to my own father and his influence in encouraging me to become a Rugby League fan, and this book is dedicated to his memory.

HARRY EDGAR (Editor, 'Rugby League Journal')

Murphy and the midas touch

(Above) Alex Murphy drops a goal for Warrington in their 1974 Wembley win over Featherstone, despite a brave attempt by Steve Nash to block the kick.
(Right) A cartoonist's impression of Murphy in Sydney during the Great Britain's Ashes-winning 1962 tour.

NOBODY who looks back on memories of Rugby League in the post-war years can fail to mention Alex Murphy who was, by far, the game's most talked about player in the days long before satellite television was invented and started trying to create personalities. Having said that, Alex was a t.v. star of his day and it was no surprise that, when the BBC's Eddie Waring was first given the opportunity to have a co-commentator offering insights alongside him, he should turn to Murphy. Eddie had got to know Alex well during the two Lions tours in 1958 and 1962 in which Murphy had run the Aussies off their feet as Great Britain retained the Ashes. He was often described as 'cocky' and there's no doubt that Alex was supremely confident in his own ability and aware of his own star quality. Eddie Waring, as the game's leading columnist with the 'Sunday Pictorial' quickly recognised that Murphy was never short of a

(Above, left) **The classic memory of the brilliant young half-back Alex Murphy - all lightening pace and brylcream - about to put the ball down between the posts for a try for St.Helens in a derby against Wigan at Knowsley Road in 1960; and** *(above, right)* **in later years, lifting the Cup for Leigh at Wembley in 1971.**

good quote and that set Alex on the way to a long association with the media after his playing days were over. Newspaper reporters knew they could rely on Alex to offer an opinion and he was never afraid of being controversial. At one time, during the 1980s, the *'Daily Mirror'* ran a regular ghosted column by him which they titled *'Murphy the Mouth'* - which hardly gave the kind of dignity a sport should have expected for a man who was, in the eyes of many, the greatest player who ever lived. But that never bothered Alex, he was always happy to talk about the game and to help publicise it.

So was Murphy the greatest player of all? Many would say yes to that, but I believe it is impossible, and futile, to try and decide who is *'best'* between totally different types of player and from very different times and eras. Suffice to say that Alex Murphy was an all-time great ... one of the greatest. My own favourite memories are of the young Alex playing for St.Helens and Great Britain on those two Lions tours and in the 1960 World Cup - lightening fast over 30 yards with his dark brylcreamed hair

bouncing in the wind. That, for me, was Murphy at his very best. But, in later years, there was another side to his game, and few who saw it can forget the gamesmanship in the 1966 Cup Final as Saints beat Wigan or the general unpleasantness of his Warrington team's behaviour as they beat Featherstone at Wembley in 1974.

The common denominator, of course, was that Murphy's team were winners. Alex was *always* a winner, the man with the Midas touch, who - after all his triumphs with Saints, including captaining them to the 'double' in 1966 - went on to player-coach Leigh to Wembley glory in 1971 and then did the same for Warrington in 1974. In later years, after hanging up his playing boots, many clubs recruited Alex as a coach - and plenty of others would have liked to recruit him - hoping he could maintain that Midas touch. But there's no doubt the Murphy magic was when he was on the field of play - the man who has had no less than three different biographies written about him, will often be remembered as controversial - but always as a winner.

Halifax star put it into print

(*Above*) **Alan Snowden as captain of the Halifax team, about to play his old club Hunslet at Parkside in January 1960. Left to right:** (*Standing*): **Sparks, Scroby, Critchley, Taylor, Thorley, Crabtree, Turnbull.** (*In front*): **Burnett, Owen, Snowden, James, Freeman and Marchant. (Note: a side with five Welshmen in it.)**

RUGBY League players who became involved in producing publications have always held a special fascination, and quite a few were familiar with the smell of printers' ink as they went about their day jobs. One was Alan Snowden, a prolific try-scoring winger for both Hunslet and Halifax, and a player who created a very special memory for me. As a young lad, with my very first autograph book in my hand, I ran on the field among a large group of kids at the end of a Whitehaven v. Halifax match, eager to get some signatures. The first player I approached was the man wearing number two in the blue and white hoops and his signature was the first ever to

(*Above*) **Action from Halifax's 1961 Cup campaign as they took on Rochdale Hornets at Thrum Hall in front of over 14,000 spectators.**

adorn that autograph book. Clearly printed it said *Alan Snowden*. I told Alan that story (and I don't know who was more embarrassed, him or me?) when he came to see me many years later at the *Open Rugby* office in Leeds. He gave me some photos, one of which is the team group at the top of this page. By that time, he was the production manager at the *Yorkshire Post* in the city, having previously

held a similar position with the *Halifax Courier*. Alan had worked his way up through the ranks of the printing trade and showed a keen interest in my work in producing a magazine. He retired from rugby in January 1962 after helping Halifax on a Cup run the previous season which took them close to Wembley. Alas, injury kept him out of the semi-final in which Halifax lost to Wigan 19-10.

Oldham a home for Cumbrians

OLDHAM played in the very first live game of Rugby League I ever attended. It was a Lancashire Cup tie at Whitehaven on 29th August 1959 and Oldham came as the holders of the trophy for the previous three years. Their run ended that day as Whitehaven beat them 23-5, which was a sign that Oldham's glorious era of the 'fifties was coming to an end. Even at such a young age back then I had three things drummed into me abut Oldham: 1) They were the best team never to get to Wembley (although Swinton fans might have something to say about that); 2) They played at a place called Watersheddings; and 3) They were instantly recognisable in newspaper pictures because they were the only team in the league to always wear dark (navy blue) shorts. And they looked great in that classic Oldham kit.

Something else which later became apparent about Oldham was that they liked players from Cumberland, and certainly signed plenty of them. A look back into the early history of the game showd that real legends like Jimmy Lomas and Joe Ferguson (both from Maryport) played for Oldham, and in August 1959 another couple of lads from the 'highside' - Ike Southward (from Ellenborough) and Geoff Robinson (from Flimby) - were Oldham's two most expensive recruits. It had taken a new world record transfer-fee of £10,650 to sign Ike from Workington Town, and Robinson

(Above) **Ike Southward bounds over for an Oldham try.**

became the most expensive forward in the game when Oldham paid £9,000 to get him from Whitehaven. Syd Little had already become an international with Oldham and other Cumbrian forwards recruited around that time were Johnny Rae (ex-Wath Brow) and Alf Mumberson (ex-Aspatria). In later years a steady flow took such as Alan Burns, Charlie McCourt and Billy McCracken from Whitehaven to Oldham - all of them forwards

(Above) **Syd Little, one of the pack stars of Oldham's great 1950s team, who won 10 Great Britain caps in consecutive Test matches. He hailed from near Carlisle and was a former RAF pilot who had formerly played Rugby Union for Harlequins, the RAF and Cumberland & Westmorland.**

(Above) **In a match against Warrington at Watersheddings in 1961, Brian Bevan manages to halt Alf Mumberson just short of the line as Johnny Noon waited in vain for a pass. On the left is Mumberson's fellow Cumbrian Johnny Rae.**

Close encounter with great Bev

(Above) **Brian Bevan proves an elusive figure for the Halifax centres Tommy Lynch and Peter Todd in the 1954 Championship Final at Maine Road, Manchester. Halifax scrum-half Stan Kielty is on the right.**

BRIAN Bevan has his place in the history of Rugby League as the greatest try scorer the game has known. His 796 tries in British Rugby League is a record that is likely to stand for ever and it is equally certain that the game, or any other sport, will never see another character quite like him. If ever there was a sporting story perfect for a movie script, the legend that was Brian Bevan would be it, because Bevan was so different and so unique it made his remarkable achievements in such a physically demanding game almost unbelievable.

Certainly many of the tries he scored appeared to be unbelievable, both to fellow players, spectators and, most especially, the opponents who were left grasping fresh air as the wonder winger ghosted past them. But Bevan's uniqueness came even more from his appearance and personality off the field, where he was so totally different from the stereotype of what a Rugby League player was expected to be - most especially an Australian player. Quiet, mysterious, shy, reclusive, introvert ... were all

words used to describe the enigma that was Brian Bevan. Team-mates who played alongside him for many years reckoned they hardly heard him speak more than a few words, and his only close confidant at the Warrington club during his 17 seasons at the club appeared to be the Wilderspool groundsman and kitman Jack Hamblett. Some reports suggested that Chris Brockbank, the former player and very experienced manager at Warrington during Bevan's first six years with the club, found it extremely difficult to communicate with the Australian winger and was frequently mystified by his behaviour - but he certainly knew what a wonderful talent and match-winner he was on the field of play.

How would Bevan have fared in the modern world of sport where reporters and t.v. interviewers expect to have players give them after-match quotes before they have even had time to get their breath back after the final whistle? And how would 21st Century coaches, with their game-plans and structures, cope with a maverick genius like Bevan?

(Above) **Very rare examples of close encounters with the great Brian Bevan. From the left: Bevan pictured arm in arm with his friend Jack Hamblett, the Warrington kitman; Bevan in his usual outfit of gaberdine coat with kit in a brown paper bag as he makes his way to the ground ready to play; and Bevan in his later years on a visit back to his native Australia and still proudly wearing his old Warrington blazer.**

Can you imagine how a young player, being thrust into the first team alongside Bevan for the first time, might feel - knowing the great man's reputation and the aura that surrounded him? I have one such revelation from Jimmy Gee who, as a young centre, found himself as a team-mate of the game's greatest try-scorer when he joined Blackpool Borough in the twilight of his career. Jimmy recalled the nerves he felt at being told he would be lining up as Brian Bevan's centre. At training during the week, and when the players met before the match on Saturday afternoon, Bevan had not spoken a word or offered any acknowledgement to the youngster who was to play centre to him. Sitting next to him in the changing room, Jimmy watched Bevan go through his ritual of taping himself and appling his bandages, still waiting for him to speak - perhaps to offer some advice or instructions, even just a word of encouragement, as to how they might try to combine on the field.

As the young centre's anxiety increased, he wondered should he break the ice and say something to Bevan - but nerves got the better of him as he thought 'who am I to start telling this legend of the game what we should, or shouldn't do ... so I kept quiet'. And then, as kick-off time approached the touch-judge's knock came on the door and the Blackpool players began to walk out. It was then that Brian Bevan finally looked at Jimmy and said, without a flicker of emotion: *'Right, son, listen to me carefully. If and when I shout for the ball you must pass it to me immediately; but on no account must you ever pass it to me unless I ask for it.'* And with that tactical pre-match planning conference over, Bevan trotted out to his position on the right wing. One of his greatest strengths as a winger, in addition to his obvious pace and elusiveness, was his anticipation. Bevan could see when a chance was materialising,

so he needed his centre to give him the ball at just the right time and he was away.

Whilst other players found it very difficult to get close to the man they called 'The Great Bev', what about the supporters? As a young fan I managed to get the rare claim to fame of being able to say I had actually met Brian Bevan and spoke to him ... and he spoke to me. Not many non-Warrington supporters could match that claim, but it was true. It happened in what turned out to be Bevan's last season with Warrington, 1961-62 - and checking back through the records I can tell you now it was on Saturday 16th September 1961, to be precise. The Wire were playing at Workington and my father told me we were making a point of going to watch this match because, in his exact words: 'This might be the last chance you get to see Brian Bevan'. He wanted his 8-year-old prodigy (me) to take that chance whilst it was still available.

So we went to Workington and, as fate would have it, were walking past the railway station on the way to Derwent Park just as the Warrington team were emerging, having travelled north by train. The players walked in a group, laughing and joking, all clad in their club blazers. Behind them was a solitary figure, a much older looking man with a bald head and wearing a heavy gaberdine coat, and carrying a brown paper parcel under his arm. 'That's Bevan,' whispered my father in hushed tones. 'Go and ask him for his autograph'. So I did, approaching the great man nervously, thrusting my autograph book and a pen towards him and stuttering 'Please can I have your autograph Mr. Bevan'. He stopped, pushed the brown paper package under his armpit, and duly signed my book. 'There you go sonny,' he said as he returned my book. Yes, the great Bevan spoke to me, and over half a century later I can still remember all four words he said!

(Left)
After his debut match for St.Helens in 1957, Tom Van Vollenhoven gets a friendly word from the Leeds full-back Pat Quinn. A Lancastrian born in Widnes, Quinn was also a former Rugby Union international who had first encountered the flying Springbok when he toured to South Africa with the British Lions in 1955. It was in that 1955 series against the British Isles that Tom Van Vollenhoven had first shot to such prominence.

Early advice for the Springbok

AMONG all the game's star names of the late 1950s and into the '60s, none came any bigger (literally) than Karel Thomas Van Vollenhoven. Along with Billy Boston and Brian Bevan, Tom was the biggest drawcard to thousands of fans at grounds across the north of England. He was worshipped by the people of St.Helens after he joined the Saints in October 1957, when he was just a shy young man arriving in a totally different environment to the one he knew in his native South Africa after a a real 'cloak and dagger' saga that would rank alongside any sport-ing drama. Telegrams had flown back and forth between south west Lancashire and Southern Africa as Wigan desperately tried to get ahead of their local rivals to aquire the signature of the young three-quarter who had been a try-scoring star for the Springboks against the British Lions in 1955. But, thanks to their *de facto* 'agent' in South Africa, a schoolteacher called Ted Higham (ironically, a Wiganer by birth), Van Vollenhoven chose the Saints. He proved to be one of the finest recruits the Rugby League game has known from the other code

(*Above*) **This was a sight that was to become very familiar for Saints fans, as their new signing Tom Van Vollenhoven sets sail down the right flank and heads for his very first try for the club at Knowsley Road against Leeds on 25th October 1957.**

and his signing prompted a flood of South African players coming to join English Rugby League clubs. From his debut against Leeds at Knowsley Road in late October 1957, it all seemed to be plain sailing for Tom on the field of play, but he was the first to pay tribute to the sound advice and assistance he got from those around him. Initially it was the Saints' coach, Jim Sullivan, who took the young Springbok under his wing and helped him to acclimatise and deal with the widespread press and media interest. Afrikaans was Van Vollenhoven's first language so, to begin with, it wasn't easy for him to communicate in English (especially English with a '*Sintellins*' accent!). Tom was grateful to his centre, the experienced tough-guy Duggie Greenall for guiding (even 'nursing') him through his early games in the new game - Duggie's best advice being 'stay on your wing' - and there was similar wise counsel from the legendary winger of the past Alf Ellaby who told Tom, as he did all aspiring wingmen, 'use your speed to stay out of trouble, the club pay you to score tries, not to get battered by the opposition'.

(*Above*) **Shortly after his arrival in St.Helens from South Africa, the young Tom Van Vollenhoven was introduced to the former great wingman Alf Ellaby, who had plenty of good advice for the new recruit.**

First taste of Wembley's magic

(Above) **Action from the 1964 Challenge Cup Final.** *(Clockwise from the top):* **1) Widnes forward Jim Measures brings down the Hull K.R. loose-forward Harry Poole; 2) The rival skippers, Vince Karalius and Harry Poole, come into direct contact; 3) Frank Collier tackles Eric Palmer watched by other Robins players Peter Flanagan, Cyril Kellett and Brian Tyson; and 4) Alan Burwell streaks away for Hull K.R.'s only try.**

THE first time I went to Wembley was in 1964, when Widnes and Hull Kingston Rovers lined up in the Challenge Cup Final. After two successive years of Wakefield Trinity triumphs at Wembley, it seemed a little strange that my first 'live and in the flesh' Cup Final should not end with Derek Turner being carried aloft with the game's most famous trophy. Instead that honour went to Vince Karalius, proudly leading his home town club 'The Chemics' to their first Challenge Cup win since the 1930s.

Going to Wembley in 1964 was made possible by the headmaster at Monkwray Junior School in Whitehaven, Mr. Lance Fitzsimmons. He was a life-long Rugby League follower whose family had an involvement in the game going right back to the early days of the Northern Union. Always keen to encourage his young pupils to take an interest in Rugby League, he had long harboured an ambition to take a group to London for the Cup Final and in 1964 that became a reality. A group of us boarded Mr. Fitzsimmons' Volkswagen camper van and headed south on our very own 'magic bus' tour.

The Final which awaited us at Wembley came as the culmination of the most incredible of Challenge Cup competitions in which an unprecedented series of draws had seen both teams - Widnes and Hull Kingston Rovers - battle their way through a testing number of replays. That included the semi-finals in which both sides had to negotiate replays (two in the case of Hull K.R. who played an epic series against Oldham).

That intense battle to get to Wembley in 1964 created an indelible image of the grandour of the Challenge Cup, as every club in the league fought through the depth of winter, into the spring, all with the burning ambition to be one of those teams walking out onto the lush turf of the Empire Stadium on a glorious day in May. Never was that more true than on Saturday 9th May, 1964, as London was bathed in warm sunshine and the thousands of fans on Wembley Way made a colourful scene with the red and white of the Robins mixed with the black and white of the Chemics. As a wide-eyed neutral, I bought rosettes in both teams' colours.

Images of Wembley in 1964 as (above left) Vince Karalius is chaired by his Widnes team as he holds the Cup aloft - just to the left in the background you can see Joe Egan, the winning coach.
(Left) Frank Collier leaves Hull K.R. defenders in his wake as he charges over for the try which helped seal the Lance Todd Trophy for him.

In those days when every daily newspaper was eager to bring the latest scoops throughout the week in the build up to Wembley, no Challenge Cup Final ever took place without some drama in the make-up of the teams. And that was certainly the case in 1964 as Hull K.R. had to call up their teenaged 'A' team prop Brian Mennell to make his Cup debut at Wembley just two days before the Final when their regular number ten John Taylor was suspended and experienced Jim Drake declared unfit. Widnes also had to make a late change when South African winger Johnny Gaydon was injured and had to be replaced by local boy Bill Thompson.

Mennell's opposite number, Frank Collier, was the oldest player in the Final at 31, and his outstanding display won him the Lance Todd trophy. It was Collier's try two minutes from full-time which sealed a 13-5 victory for Widnes. After a dour first half in which both teams struggled to break free from defences, the Chemics held a two-nil lead, but the second 40 minutes brought plenty of attacking thrills. Alan Briers and Frank Myler scored tries for Widnes and Alan Burwell replied with a superb arching run for Hull K.R. - the moment I still remember most clearly from the 1964 Final. Almost 50 years later I talked about this Final with

(Above) The teenaged front-row-forward Brian Mennell, making his Cup debut for Hull K.R. at Wembley, is surrounded by the Widnes defence with referee Dickie Thomas keeping a close watch.

a couple of the men who played in it. Jim Measures, the Widnes second-rower, remembered the match being played with a smaller than normal brown ball: "We never got a chance to practise with it - they just threw it to us as we were walking out." And Graham Paul, the 'Cornish Express' on the wing for Hull K.R. was disappointed he didn't get much chance to show his speed: "It wasn't much of a game." Believe me Graham, for a boy at his very first Wembley Final it was an unforgettable game.

Castleford's home town class made television stars

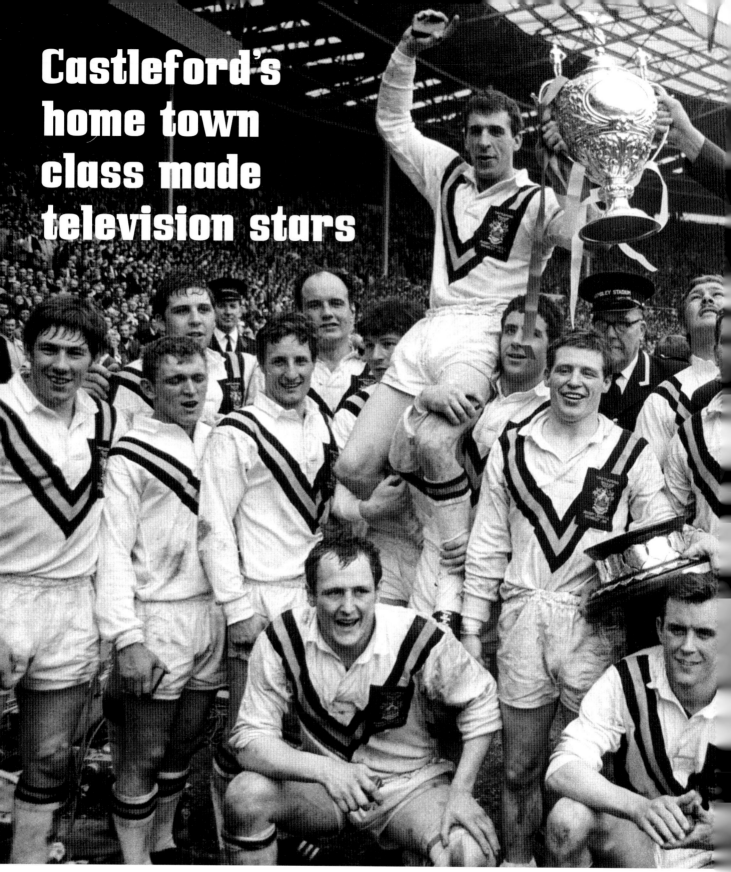

(Above) **Alan Hardisty carried aloft with the Challenge Cup by his Castleford team at Wembley in 1969.**

CASTLEFORD'S catch-phrase of 'Classy Cas' was born in the mid 1960s as a new generation of Rugby League fans came to see the Yorkshire team as one of the game's 'glamour' sides. Certainly they were colourful, clad in bright golden jerseys, and they had talented young players emerging who played a sparkling brand of rugby. But the key to the rise in Castleford's popularity was down to the growing power and influence of television. In 1965 the BBC, already regularly covering Rugby League on their Saturday afternoon 'Grandstand' programme, launched a new competition to be broadcast on their fledgling BBC Two channel. The 'Floodlit Trophy' gave Rugby League a slice of prime-time television

(Above) **The Castleford team in 1965-66, just as the era of 'Classy Cas' was beginning to emerge. As an example of the local talent available then at Wheldon Road, this picture shows both Alan Hardisty and Roger Millward together in the same team. Hardisty, the captain, stayed and Millward left for Hull K.R.**

on Tuesday nights and Castleford, the first Yorkshire club to install floodlights in the 'sixties (notwithstanding Bradford Northern's previous version of floodlighting at Odsal in the 1950s), took full advantage of this chance to enjoy publicity on a national stage. Castleford won the 'Floodlit Trophy' in its first three seasons, beating St.Helens, Swinton and Leigh respectively in the finals, and the Cas' captain Alan Hardisty reckoned that television coverage was a massive turning point in the town's interest in Rugby League and the club's reputation throughout the game and beyond.

On Tuesday nights the town would come alive as people flocked around any available t.v. sets to watch the rugby - and I can tell you this wasn't just in Castleford, but in towns all across the north of England. The Cas' players became instantly recognisable personalities with the biggest star names, initially, being Hardisty and his half-back partner Keith Hepworth. As always, the BBC commentator Eddie Waring was keen to promote personalities in the game, and he recognised the star quality of Hardisty. Eddie would tell viewers that they should keep their eye on Hardisty because 'you might not see him for 79 minutes and then, in the very last minute, he'll win the game'. And Eddie was right.

For Rugby League fans who knew a bit about the game, that became a very familiar script. Hardisty was the supreme opportunist who could pounce, out of nowhere - back up and be through a

(Above) **Castleford's Clive Dickinson challenged by Bill Ramsey of Leeds as Dennis Hartley keeps an eye on things in this clash in the later 1960s.**

gap and under the posts, or take an interception. No individual better illustrated the tag of 'Classy Cas' than Alan Hardisty, one of the finest footballers the game has known, but much of the credit for the style developed by Castleford went to their former coach Harry Street. He had taken over at Wheldon Road in 1958 when Cas' had spent years struggling in the lower reaches of the league table, and turned them into a successful and attractive team. And it was all built on local players, products of the schools and juniors, who provided Castleford with a conveyer belt of talent throughout the 'sixties.

Barrow's hero everybody's idol

(Above) **The moment Willie Horne and his Barrow team took the applause of the Craven Park crowd as they entered the field to a guard of honour given by the Leigh players on the Monday after Barrow's win at Wembley in the 1955 Cup Final. Willie and his boys had just got home after completing their train journey back from London and an open-top bus parade through the Furness area back into the centre of Barrow.**

BARROW played a major part in my Rugby League education as the first 'away' ground I got to visit. And Craven Park had a special atmosphere, covered on all four sides and safe in the knowledge it had played host to one of the finest teams in the league when Willie Horne was their stand-off and captain. Rarely can any individual have been such a talisman for the people of his home town than Willie was to the good folk of Barrow-in-Furness.

Willie's testimonial brochure was titled *'An idol of the crowd'* and he certainly was an idol to my father who, like so many star-struck fans, took his son to Willie's sports-shop in Barrow to buy his first rugby ball and first pair of football-boots, whilst enjoying the chance to chat with the great man himself. The wizard who wore the number six jersey for Barrow, Lancashire, England and Great Britain, was a very shy man, known for his kindness and generosity - something I can vouch for personally. Of course, Barrow had many other wonderful players during Willie's time, and in the early 1960s another star emerged in the flying winger Bill Burgess - so many times Burgess broke the heart of my team with his match-winning tries.

(Above) **Bill Burgess, Barrow's flyer on the wing.**

(Pictured) The one and only Billy Boston in action for Wigan against Hull in the 1959 Cup Final at Wembley. Since the day the great man retired Wigan seemed to be on a search for 'the new Billy'.

Henderson was the new star

Henderson Gill

and did 'a bit of a boogie'

WIGAN have had many stars but none as big as Billy Boston. Certainly for my generation, and I suspect most others, Rugby League in Britain has never had a more famous player than Billy, whose career at Central Park began in a blaze of publicity and was sprinkled with stardust for ever after. Billy, the boy from Tiger Bay, left a wonderful legacy for Wigan with his try-scoring records and the special place he holds in the history of the whole town, not just the rugby club. But he also left Wigan with the massive headache of their never-ending search for a successor who could have the same effect on their fans. It seemed every new winger signed by Wigan was going to be the 'new Billy Boston', when everybody really knew that nobody could have the same impact as Billy. Among those who carried that burden was Green Vigo, from South Africa and with a name every bit as exotic as Billy Boston. And then along came Henderson Gill, bright , bubbly and a real crowd pleaser. Henderson was one the game's biggest stars of the 1980s, and who can forget his magical tries at Wembley in 1985 (followed by *the* grin) and then in the Test match in Sydney in 1988 when the immortal line *'he does a bit of a boogie'* was uttered, to be associated with him for ever.

The Chemics in the first of their famous Wembley sequence in 1975 as *(left)* Ray Dutton kicks one of his goals and *(above)* Jim Mills brings the Cup home to Widnes and *(below)* riding over the Runcorn bridge.

Widnes were the Cup kings

WHEN historians tell stories of the great teams and successful eras in Rugby League, there's one which I always think slips under the radar and doesn't get the full recognition it deserves. That is the story of Widnes, who became the Cup kings across an incredible decade of success spanning from 1975 to 1984. In those ten years the Chemics played in no less than seven Challenge Cup Finals, winning four and finishing runners-up in three.

Some Widnes players, well known for their sense of humour, quipped that Wembley was their home ground, and certainly the Twin Towers got used to an invasion of the black and white colours almost every year. Widnes had always been known as a team built on local players and that was certainly the case when they kicked off this glorious era with victory in the 1975 Cup Final over Warrington with no less than 11 local lads in their team - the

only two 'imports' being Welshman Jim Mills at prop and a guest player from Australia on the wing in Chris Anderson. For the record the Widnes team at Wembley in 1975 was: Ray Dutton; Alan Prescott, Mick George, Mal Aspey, Chris Anderson; Eric Hughes, Reg Bowden; Jim Mills, Keith Elwell, Barry Sheridan, John Foran, Mick Adams, Doug Laughton. Most of those players would return many times to Wembley and appear in other cup finals.

The Lance Todd Trophy award in 1975 went to full-back Ray Dutton, in recognition of his marvellous goal-kicking (he landed five, plus a drop-goal) which kept the Chemics in front of their rivals. Warrington went into that game as the Cup holders, but were left well beaten by a team the Widnes coach Vince Karalius was keen to promote as 100% fit athletes. It was a proud day for Vinty as his boys brought the Cup back to home-town Widnes.

Days of glory for the Town

(Above) **Billy Ivison on the ball for Workington Town against Featherstone Rovers in the 1952 Cup Final at Wembley with his centre Tony Paskins in support.**

IN Cumberland tales were passed down from father to son about Gus Risman and his successful Workington Town team. No man in the county was held in higher regard than Gus who, having arrived at the new Workington club as they began their second season in 1946, quickly built a side that would bring the game's highest honours. Their sheer quality meant it was always an impossible task for future generations to live up to what the Cumbrian public had seen from Risman's team. I was regaled with stories of players like Tony Paskins, the powerful centre from Australia and his second-row mate Johnny Mudge; Johnny Lawrenson, the lightening quick winger who was a current international when Workington signed him from Wigan; and Billy Ivison, the scrum-capped loose-forward who could run and handle like a centre and worked on a brewery truck during the week. This was the team my father idolised as a young man, and he loved to tell the story about Gus saying his greatest moment had come in the 1951 Championship Final when, midway throught the second half, he realised that Town could not be beaten and were going to be crowned champions. Many years later when I had the privilege of meeting Gus Risman, I asked him if that story was true - he smiled and told me it was.

(Above) **The moment captain Gus Risman held the Cup for Workington at Wembley in 1952, carried aloft by Tony Paskins and 'Pongo' Wareing. Other Town players in the picture are Johnny Lawrenson on the right with 'Happy' Wilson and Jackie Thomas at the front.**

Swinton ghosts of Station Road

(Above) Station Road not very full in the late 1950s as Swinton stand-off George Parkinson races over for a try against Liverpool City, leaving Ray Hockenhull in his wake.
(Right) A very different atmosphere with over 30,000 packed in for the infamous Test match 'massacre' in 1963 - Swinton favourite John Stopford, on his home ground, tries to evade the Kangaroo defenders.

STATION Road was a cathedral of Rugby League and always a place where the ghosts of the past seemed to be present. For this was the place where, on 4th January 1930, in the first Test match to be played there at the vast new ground in the suburbs of Manchester, England and Australia fought out a nil-nil draw and the famous 'Chimpy' Busch no-try had taken place. Thirty-three years later, just as the 'swinging sixties' were being unleashed and Swinton were becoming the game's trendiest team again, another seminal moment in the history of Test football unfolded at Station Road when Australia hammered an injury hit British team by an unthinkable 50 points to 12, and so won the Ashes on British soil at long last. Four years later, in 1967, they did it again on an icy pitch and with snow falling on them. Those winter moments are part of international Rugby League history, but Swinton fans had much happier memories of springtime in 1963 and '64 as their very own Lions were crowned Champions and captain Albert Blan held the trophy aloft. Swinton were popular winners throughout the game, their quality remains admired forever.

Rovers - day of the underdog

(*Above*) **Lance Todd Trophy winner in 1983, Featherstone's David Hobbs. His two tries put Rovers on the way to a shock victory over Hull. (*Left*) Action from that 1983 Cup Final as Rovers' forward Peter Smith gets the ball moving - a former team-mate, Charlie Stone looks on.**

OF all the Challenge Cup Finals seen at Wembley, one that holds most vivid memories is the 1983 match between Featherstone and Hull. Not for the quality of the football, which wasn't a patch on several other Finals, most notably the 1985 classic between Wigan and Hull. But the sheer emotion of the 1983 Final provided incredible sporting drama as the Rovers, as one of the biggest underdogs ever at Wembley, well and truly had their day.

Because Featherstone was a mining 'village' with a population of around just 14,000, they were used to being portrayed as 'Davids' playing against 'Goliaths', but the Rovers had built an impressive Challenge Cup record with two previous Wembley wins, in 1967 over Barrow and 1973 over Bradford Northern. In both of those Cup Finals many saw Featherstone as pre-match favourites, but that was not the case in 1983 when they lined up against an expensively put together Hull team who were the Cup holders from the previous season and had just been crowned Rugby League Champions for 1982-83. Meanwhile, Featherstone has finished in 12th position, narrowly avoiding relegation. Hull's line-up at Wembley included seven Great Britain Test caps and three Kiwi internationals, and they faced a Rovers team of all local lads, with the only 'import' being centre

(*Above*) **Happy Featherstone Rovers players do a lap of honour at Wembley in 1967 led by their captain Malcolm Dixon - it was the first time Rovers had won the Cup.**

Steve Quinn from faraway York. And it was Quinn who became the match-winner with his accurate goal-kicking - this included a penalty goal from a difficult angle in the last minute. It was a foul by former Rover Charlie Stone on Peter Smith which brought the penalty, with the scores level at 12-all. Steve Quinn held his nerve to make it 14-12 and win the Cup, although he admitted he wasn't aware there was so little time left, otherwise his legs would have probably turned to rubber!

Trinity's unstoppable Cup run

(Above) **The great Wakefield Trinity team in 1959-60. Left to right:** *(Standing):* **John Etty, Don Metcalfe, Jack Wilkinson, Alan Skene, Fred Smith, Keith Holliday, Harold Poynton, Neil Fox.** *(In front):* **David Wakefield, Albert Firth, Malcolm Sampson, Derek Turner (captain), Don Vines. Four players missing from this picture played for Trinity in the 1960 Cup Final: Gerry Round, Ken Rollin, Geoff Oakes and Les Chamberlain.**

WAKEFIELD Trinity emerged as the game's leading club as the decade of the 'sixties dawned, winning the first of their three Challenge Cups in four years in 1960. And that Trinity team made a massive impression on people way beyond the confines of their own 'merrie city'. Their 1960 Cup run was an epic story, not least because it marked their arrival at the top and gave vindication to the steady team-building which had been going on at Wakefield, notably the signing of the experienced Oldham trio John Etty, Don Vines and Derek Turner, along with Jack Wilkinson from Halifax. In addition Trinity had uncovered a South African gem in Alan Skene and had a solid foundation of talented local boys coming into their prime, among them Neil Fox, Harold Poynton and Keith Holliday. But getting to Wembley in 1960 was no easy ride as Wakefield had to negotiate the toughest of routes with all of their first three rounds away from home. It all

(Above) **John Etty with the Cup - his tries in the early rounds at St.Helens and Widnes played a big part in getting Trinity on the road to Wembley.**

started at Knowsley Road where St.Helens, the reigning League Champions, were hot favourites to get to Wembley themselves. With winger John Etty in fine form, both on attack and in defence, Trinity upset the Saints to cause quite a stir with a 15-10 win. In the second round it was away in Lancashire again, this time at Widnes, and once more a try by Etty proved crucial as Wakefield edged through 5-2.

And so it was on to the quarter-final and another away draw, this time up north in Cumberland at Whitehaven. This was where the powerful aura of Wakefield Trinity in that era made its huge impression on me, because I was one of over 18,600 souls packed like sardines onto the old wooden terraces of Whitehaven's Recreation Ground to see them. It was 19th March 1960, a cold day when a bitter chill blew through the hopes of my local team of progressing to the semi-final as they were ground into submission by Wakefield.

(Above) Ken Rollin on the attack against Hull at Wembley in 1960 with winger Fred Smith in support. Rollin scored a brilliant solo try to set Wakefield on their way and (below) receives the congratulations of his team-mates including Jack Wilkinson and Geoff Oakes.
(Right) Trinity's Alan Skene tackles Hull centre Nan Halifihi as Derek Turner and Fred Smith keep a close eye on things.

Trinity owed so much to their captain Derek 'Rocky' Turner who, when the going got toughest, just rolled his sleeves up (literally!) and led from the front, scoring two tries through sheer determination. Many years later, the Whitehaven player-coach Eppie Gibson bemoaned the fact that his team had drawn Wakefield in that quarter-final - 'If it had been anybody else, we would have made the semi, but that Trinity side was unbeatable'. And so it proved as captain 'Rocky' went on to lift the Cup. Their drawing power was shown by the size of the crowds who watched them on their way to Wembley: 29,371 at St.Helens; 18,773 at Widnes; 18,650 at Whitehaven; and then 55,935 against Featherstone in the semi-final.

Happy hero who saved a club

(Above, left) **Bill Holliday in action for Whitehaven in his last home game for the club before his transfer to Hull Kingston Rovers. This was on 19th December 1964, against Wigan, and the other Whitehaven men in the picture are Les Moore and Jim Wilson, as Wigan's prop John Barton grapples with Holliday.**
(Above, right) **Bill playing for Great Britain against France at Perpignan in 1966 as a familiar foe in the shape of Marcel Bescos gives chase. Holliday's future Swinton team-mate Ken Gowers is in support.**

YOUNG Rugby League fans all have their childhood heroes, and mine was Bill Holliday. Captain of my home town club, a fine forward and goal-kicker who became a truly inspirational figure during the early part of the 1964-65 season when he led Whitehaven to a club record nine match winning streak. Trouble was ... it almost bankrupted the club which, for some time, had been on sticky ground financially. Nine consecutive weeks of finding winning pay, but no dramatic increase in gates, meant Whitehaven were perilously close to being wound up. Their only solution was to sell their greatest asset, and that was Bill Holliday. The man known by his nickname 'Happy' did not ask for a transfer, but he agreed to move for the sake of helping the club secure its future in January 1965.

By this time, Holliday had become hot property after making his Test debut in France and being Great Britain's best forward in a disappointing defeat to the French. Most of the top clubs were keen to sign him and, eventually, it was Hull K.R. who got Bill to become a 'Robin' and paid a club record fee of £8,000 to do it. That cash saved the Whitehaven club, and 'Happy' truly was a hero to his home town. Hull K.R. never regretted splashing out so much to sign Bill as he played a massive role in making the Robins one of the strongest teams in the league, and he went on to captain Great Britain in the 1967 Ashes. Holliday later also captained both Swinton and Rochdale.

(Above) **Bill Holliday looks to get the ball away playing for Whitehaven in 1962 at home to Widnes.**

Reminders of another time

On this page we illustrate just a few of the ways we can preserve Rugby League's history and keep alive memories of the game's great events and achievements. Printed documents in the form of programmes and brochures are the classic mode of preservation and here we see the changing format of Challenge Cup Final programmes and a reminder of two of the game's now long gone competitions, plus that familiar friend, the 'Eddie Waring Annual'. The medals on the left are those awarded to winners of the Challenge Cup and the Championship and the whole display is set against the backdrop of Neil Fox, the game's greatest points scorer, whose records will, surely, never be overtaken.

THE QUEEN'S SILVER JUBILEE
RUGBY LEAGUE CHALLENGE CUP FINAL
RL
SATURDAY 13TH MAY 1978
Kick-off: 3 p.m.
LEEDS v ST. HELENS
Wembley Stadium

YORKSHIRE CHALLENGE CUP FINAL
CASTLEFORD v HULL K.R.
SATURDAY
at BELLE VUE WAKEFIELD
PRICE 10p

THE RUGBY LEAGUE CHALLENGE CUP COMPETITION
FINAL TIE
HULL KINGSTON ROVERS
v
WIDNES
SATURDAY MAY 9th 1964 Kick-off 3 p.m.
WEMBLEY
EMPIRE STADIUM
OFFICIAL PROGRAMME - - - ONE SHILLING

RUGBY LEAGUE CHALLENGE CUP COMPETITION
FINAL TIE
SATURDAY · MAY 3RD 1947
Kick-off 3·30 P.M.
EMPIRE STADIUM
WEMBLEY
LEEDS v BRADFORD NORTHERN
OFFICIAL PROGRAMME · SIXPENCE

EDDIE WARING
RUGBY LEAGUE ANNUAL
No. 6   1964-5   2/6

Player's Nº6 Trophy Final
CENTRAL PARK, WIGAN, FEB 9th 1974 KICK OFF 3pm
ROCHDALE HORNETS
v
WARRINGTON
OFFICIAL PROGRAMME   PRICE 10p

Flying the flag for old England

(Pictured) **Geoff Pimblett, the St.Helens full-back, representing England on his home ground at Knowsley Road as they thrashed Wales 60-13 in May 1978. School teacher Pimblett kicked a record nine goals as England also ran in 14 tries to romp home in the sun and clinch the Jean Galia trophy. Note the all white jersey with red and blue shoulder stripes, which was the England kit worn between 1978 and '81, and distinguished them from the traditional Great Britain outfit.**

WHEN it comes to international Rugby League the Great Britain team was always the pinnacle of our game - even when the British team was called 'England' or the 'Northern Union' in the years pre-1947 when the Great Britain tag was officially adopted. Going on tour as the Lions, or playing Test matches on home soil, Great Britain - wearing their trademark white jerseys with the red and blue vee - were the standard bearers for Rugby League. But there was also a place for the England team, playing European internationals against France and Wales.

Rugby League always liked to have an annual European Championship, but its fluctuating existence usually depended on having enough Welsh players to be able to put together a competitive team representing the Principality. During the 1970s some of England's most memorable games in the European Championship included their most controversial encounters against France. Both England and Wales had played as separate teams in the 1975 World Championship, and in the years between 1977 and 1981 the annual clashes between the

Scenes from two of England's toughest battles in France. *(Far left)* At Narbonne in 1980, English scrum-half Alan Redfearn is harrassed by his opposite number Ivan Greseque, as French hooker Henri Daniel put his knee into an English forward in the scrum. *(Left)* England captain Roger Millward, on the bench after being battered out of the game at Toulouse in 1978.

English and the French produced enough fireworks to make Guy Fawkes stop in his tracks - and I witnessed them all first hand.

It all began in the spring of 1977 at Carcassonne where France ran riot to beat England 28-15 to clinch the European Championship title and with it the Jean Galia trophy, in honour of the founder of the French game. That was my first experience of Rugby League in France and of watching England play on overseas soil. The French that day lived up to every single cliché in the book - playing with the sun on their backs, they played some spectacular off-the-cuff rugby which provided the beauty to go with the inevitable brutality. I had rarely seen such blatant violence in a game of Rugby League before, which included a stand-up fight between England's Mike Coulman and France's Jean-Jacques Cologni and a terrible battering inflicted upon the English captain Roger Millward. England that day were coached by Peter Fox and this defeat in Carcassonne, coupled with the previous loss at home to Wales, effectively put an end to Peter's hopes of taking the Great Britain team down-under for the 1977 World Cup at the end of that season.

In 1978 England were back in France, this time in the magnificent municipal Stadium in Toulouse, and this time with a steely determination to gain revenge over the French. With a pack bolstered by the inclusion of some tough and experienced forwards like Mick Harrison, George Nicholls and Len Casey, plus Steve Nash playing like an extra forward at scrum-half, England met fire with fire and

were able to win a close encounter 13-11. Frank Myler was the England coach that year, and they followed the victory in Toulouse with a crushing 60-13 win over Wales in a game played at St.Helens in baking hot conditions at the end of the season. That match had originally been scheduled to be played at Swansea in February, but heavy snow meant it had to be postponed.

In 1979, with the Anglo-French match played on home soil at Warrington, there were less controversies surrounding the game and certainly less headaches and bruises for the English team. It was a decider for the title as both nations also beat Wales, and France came to Warrington confident of victory after they had recently beaten Australia in two Tests to clinch a series win over the Kangaroos. But England, captained by Brian Lockwood, held the visitors at bay and were able to win 12-6 and retain the Jean Galia trophy.

The 1980 France-England game at Narbonne achieved a real infamy in the annals of international Rugby League. The English were incensed at the violence of the French, which resulted in prop Keith Rayne having to go to hospital after being kicked in a scrum; and the French were just as angry about the refereeing of Englishman Billy Thompson - an anger which led to the official having to be locked in the dressing rooms after the game whilst an ugly mob outside bayed for his blood. Amid all this mayhem, England (coached by Eric Ashton) prevailed to win 4-2, and the aftermath brought calls from RFL Council member Bill Oxley to scrap all matches against the French until they stopped the violence.

France took their revenge for Narbonne the following year, 1981, when a partisan display of refereeing by Guy Cattaneo helped them to a 5-1 win over England at Headingley, and with it the European Championship. England then were coached by Johnny Whiteley, who was also the Great Britain coach. It was certainly an era when flying the flag for England meant some bruising battles for the players with no little blood spilled.

Memories made of this

Why top league players train on BOVRIL

Bovril for fitness without fatness

Memories were made of this as *(above)* we see a typical scene from a misty winter's night game with steam rising from the packs and, even more typically, referee Gerry Kershaw getting into the middle to show the front-rows who was the boss. This was a John Player Trophy match between Hull K.R. and Halifax in January 1985 and you can almost smell that wonderul aroma of Bovril, pies, pipe-tobacco and wintergreen. Did top players really train on Bovril? The advert in the 1964 Cup Final programme says they did. In sharp contrast to all this was international rugby and the presence of a touring team in the autumn, and none came as more of a breath of fresh air than the 1980 Kiwis - the last of the great amateur touring teams. One of their best was Gary Prohm, pictured *(below)* in Test action against Great Britain. Prohm became a star for Hull K.R.

(*Above*) A fond farewell to Central Park from two Wigan and Great Britain legends, Eric Ashton and Billy Boston, as the grand old ground closed in 1999.

Anglo-Australian rivalry underpinned everything in Rugby League since the first Ashes encounter in 1908, and these more modern memories illustrate just how strongly that rivalry continued to burn. (*At the top of the page*) A moment of triumph for England over Australia at Wembley in the 1995 World Cup as Paul Newloves raises arms in delight at the final whistle. (*Above*) David Topliss leads Great Britain out against the 1982 Kangaroo 'Invincibles' at Headingley. (*Left*) A landmark day in Ashes history in 1986 as the first Test was played at Old Trafford - British forwards Kevin Ward, Ian Potter and Andy Goodway attack.

Greats of Fartown won Yorkshire Cup

'Hurrah for the Claret and Gold'

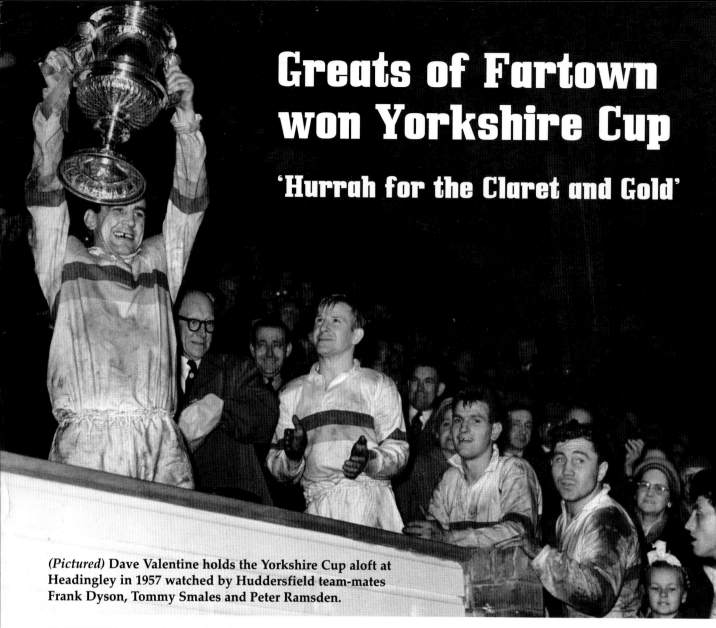

(Pictured) **Dave Valentine holds the Yorkshire Cup aloft at Headingley in 1957 watched by Huddersfield team-mates Frank Dyson, Tommy Smales and Peter Ramsden.**

FARTOWN was always Rugby League 'royalty'. Tales passed down of the legendary Harold Wagstaff, Douglas Clark, Albert Rosenfeld and their 'Team of All Talents', followed later by the exciting post World War Two side packed with stars from around the globe, have given Huddersfield a special place in the history of the game. That royalty was bequeathed the special gift of being able to wear the classic claret and gold colours. Some things should never be tampered with and Huddersfield's kit, like those of several other clubs which provide a similar unique 'selling point', is a gift any professional marketeer worth his salt would kill for.

And Huddersfield had the most famous and immediately recognisable 'alternative' kit in Rugby League when colour clashes led them to wear their white jersey with a single claret and gold hoop (as seen in the picture, above). This was on the occasion of their victory over York in the Yorkshire Cup Final at Headingley in October 1957 - Huddersfield's first major trophy for four years and a lone taste of glory sandwiched in an extended run of disappointment which lasted all the way to their Championship win

in 1962. That glorious achievement, which came when Fartown defeated Wakefield Trinity in the Final at Odsal just seven days after losing to them in the Challenge Cup Final at Wembley, was a quite a triumph both for their captain Tommy Smales and coach Dave Valentine.

It was nine years on from when Huddersfield had won the Challenge Cup, beating St.Helens in the 1953 Final at Wembley. That victory kind of put the icing on the cake of Fartown's glorious era after the war, and it was followed by a gradual decline as many of the stars retired and the claret and gold's reputation for being the outstanding footballing team in the league began to slip. Dave Valentine was one man who maintained a link with the glory days as the second half of the 1950s unfolded - the mighty Scotsman, inspirational captain of Great Britain in the first World Cup tournament, was still there as the Yorkshire Cup was captured in 1957 but, subequently, a broken ankle was to spell the end of his playing career. That left younger stars like the trio pictured above - Frank Dyson, Tommy Smales and Peter Ramsden - to take Fartown to future triumphs.

Days by the seaside

Blackpool Borough enjoyed a couple of days in the limelight when they opened both the 1978 Kangaroo and 1980 Kiwi tours. *(Below)* Captain John Corcoran and Phil Holmes lead the Borough out against New Zealand, and the pictures *(left)* show the Aussies in action at Borough Park, with Craig Young and Norman Turley the two players in possession of the ball.

NO book of Rugby League memories would be complete without a visit to Blackpool because, for many fans of a certain age, a trip to the seaside was their favourite away match. Founded in 1954 and playing first at the St.Anne's Road Stadium, Blackpool Borough tried manfully throughout their thirty-three year history to establish the game on the Fylde coast in what was the north of England's favourite holiday resort. I can remember the sheer joy and optimism that swept across the league when Blackpool opened their brand new ground, Borough Park, in 1963. They even had the great Brian Bevan in their team when they did it. The Borough, in their tangerine, black and white colours, were always popular, and many of their players came from the Wigan area eager to get a chance of first team rugby. But their best ever discovery actually came from St.Helens, a certain scrum-half called Tommy Bishop. It was a sad day when Blackpool were forced out of Borough Park in 1987.

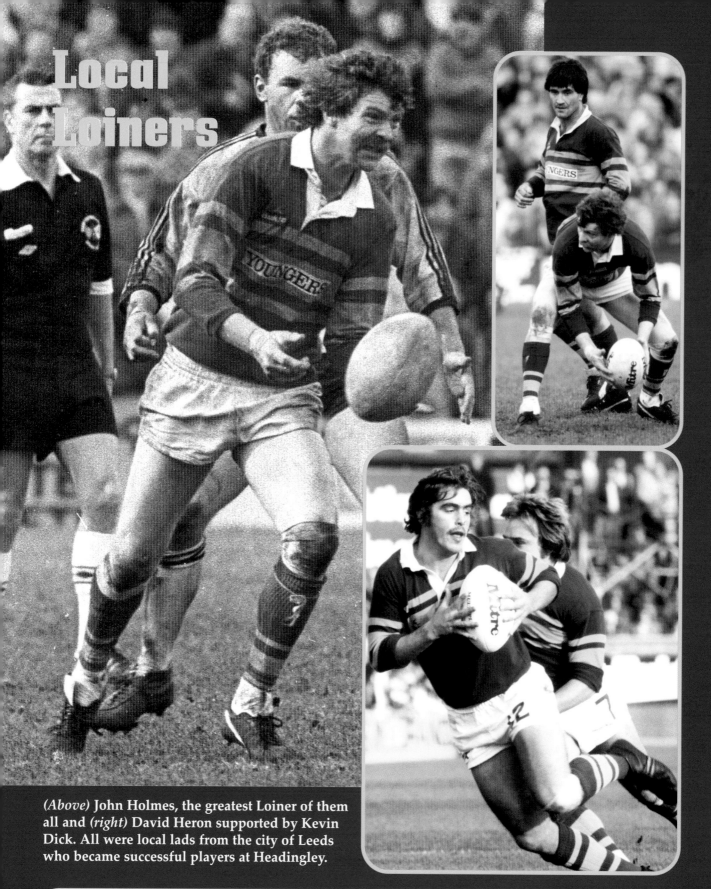

Local Loiners

(*Above*) **John Holmes, the greatest Loiner of them all and** (*right*) **David Heron supported by Kevin Dick. All were local lads from the city of Leeds who became successful players at Headingley.**

LEEDS always had a reputation as the glamour club of Rugby League, although I'm sure that had a lot to do with the prestige of their Headingley home with it being a Test cricket ground as well as a rugby stadium. And Leeds was a big city club in a game built mostly on small towns. For a long time, going back to pre-War years, Leeds had searched far and wide to recruit star players, with no shortage of Australians and Welshmen donning the blue and amber colours. That continued into the 1940s when a new group of adventurers came from the southern hemisphere to Headingley: Arthur Clues, Ted Verrenkamp, Bob McMaster and Len Kenny from Australia, plus full-back Bert

Cooke from New Zealand. The Welshmen included stand-off Dickie Williams (who went on to captain Great Britain) and the golden boy, Lewis Jones. But it always seemed that whenever Leeds tasted some of their much craved success, they did it with a strong backbone of local lads in their team.

I remember when I first met Joe Warham, the manager of the first ever Leeds side to win the Championship in 1960-61. Even more than that title victory, Joe was immensely proud of the work he had done in scouting, recruiting and encouraging the many young players who had gone on to become the outstanding Loiners team of the later 'sixties - these included the great half-back pair of Mick Shoebottom and Barry Seabourne, centres Syd Hynes and Bernard Watson, and the magical wing duo Alan Smith and John Atkinson. Five of that half dozen would also be part of the triumphant 1970 British Lions touring team.

It is interesting to note that of the thirteen Leeds players in the 1968 'Watersplash' Final at Wembley, twelve were products of Yorkshire junior rugby, with the only exception being full-back Bev Risman, born in Lancashire and raised in Cumberland. That team also illustrated that Leeds were no strangers to signing top players from other clubs - something which didn't make them too popular with some of their neighbours. In their pack at Wembley in 1968 were three Hunslet men, Ken and Albert Eyre (albeit Albert came to Leeds via Keighley) and Bill Ramsey. Wakefield Trinity also had cause to rue the way Leeds could 'mop up' some of their best players - they had lost Don Robinson in the 1950s, and that pathway continued through each successive era with such as Bob Haigh, then the Rayne twins, all the way to modern times and Gareth Ellis, all moving to Headingley.

But it was signing local juniors and seeing them develop into top players which gave most satisfaction to Joe Warham, and another great generation came through, including John Holmes, David Ward, Graham Eccles, Steve Pitchford and Kevin Dick, which brought more success for Leeds in the 1970s. For me, it was always good to be able to spot a young player before he became a professional, and

(Above) **One who wasn't a local at Leeds was the former Springbok Wilf Rosenberg, pictured here making his debut at Headingley versus Barrow on 28th February 1959. He left South Africa to study dentistry at Leeds University and went on to set a new Leeds post-war record of 44 tries in the club's first Championship winning season of 1960-61.**

see him go on to achieve all his potential and become a star - and that happened with two of the Leeds players I admired most from my time in the city. The first was John Holmes, whom I first saw playing for the Yorkshire Schoolboys at Whitehaven as a 15-year-old. He was head and shoulders above all the other boys on the field and by then it was known that he was going to be signed by Leeds, although I know Bradford Northern also tried very hard to sign John and offered him more money than Leeds. But John was from Kirkstall and all he ever wanted to do was play for the Loiners - and he became the greatest Loiner of them all, playing a record 625 first team games in a career that spanned fully 22 years. My other favourite Leeds player was David Heron, a classic loose-forward who first came to my notice playing for Hunslet Parkside in the BARLA Under-18s Cup. Dave was a great footballer who made every coaching manual come to life. Along with Steve Pitchford, who - appropriately enough - worked in a tank factory at Crossgates, and Kevin Dick, Roy Dickinson and Graham Eccles from the other side of the city, they were all Leeds boys who brought much success to the Loiners.

The new taste of Sponsorship

(Above) **Action from the one and only Captain Morgan Trophy Final, at Salford in 1974, as Featherstone Rovers' Mike Smith, closely supported by Paul Coventry, faces the challenge of Warrington's John Bevan.**

SPONSORSHIP is now accepted as an essential part of modern day sport and Rugby League, as it has been in so many things, was a pioneer of this in Britain. So called 'commercial' sponsorship was first sighted in British Rugby League back in 1961 when the Kiwi tour was supported by Mackeson, with gold watches going to the players who scored most points against the touring New Zealanders.

This was followed by the Mackeson Contest, for the teams who scored most points, and later the Mackeson Golden Ball. Mackeson's sponsorship came to an end in 1970, by which time the support of John Player was gathering momentum after tobacco company support had begun with Benson & Hedges sponsoring awards on the 1965 Kiwi tour. Sponsorship took a major step when, in the 1971-72 season, the Players No. 6 competition was launched, the first time that a new knock-out competition had been set up specifically to provide sponsors with their own tournament.

The key to that support from John Player was the fact that their competition was able to attract live television coverage on Saturday afternoons on the BBC, and during the 'seventies Rugby League became awash with sponsors trying to jump on that bandwagon, which included both County Cups being sponsored by breweries.

However, as if to prove you can have too much of a good thing, Rugby League went one step too far when, the promise of a new lucrative sponsorship - this time from Captain Morgan rum - persuaded it to launch yet another new knockout competition in the 1973-74 season. The Captain Morgan Trophy featured just 16 teams, the winners of the first round of the Lancashire and Yorkshire Cups. It culminated with a final, between Featherstone Rovers and Warrington, at The Willows, Salford on 26th January 1974. The Wire won a dour game 4-nil to take the winners' prize of £3,000. And the Captain Morgan Trophy was never played for again.

Leigh's international stars

LEIGH produced two of the most talented of all British players I have had the privilege of seeing, yet both are hardly mentioned when others nominate the game's 'best ever' international players. I am referring to John Woods and Des Drummond, who both had the bad luck of being around at the wrong time when it came to international football. They were at their peak during that decade between 1978 and 1988 when Great Britain couldn't win a single Test match against Australia - and by the time they finally managed it, in the third Test in Sydney in 1988, both John and Des had gone from the national team. Leigh fans, of course, knew all about their abilities.

(*Above*) Leigh players Jimmy Ledgard and Frank Kitchen receive their international caps after playing their part in Great Britain's 1954 World Cup triumph. Presenting the caps is Mr. Bob Anderton, who was originally named as the British team manager but had to step down and miss the tournament because of illness.

(*Above*) Des Drummond in action for Leigh.

They had been key players in the club's famous Championship title wining side of 1981-82 and, as a sign of just how much Des Drummond was appreciated, he did win 24 Test caps. But John Woods went grossly unappreciated - he was, in my view, one of the best stand-offs this country has ever produced, yet he managed only seven Test caps between 1979 and 1987. He hardly ever was given the chance to play for Great Britain in his natural position, making his debut as a makeshift full-back in the nightmare in Brisbane first Test on the 1979 tour, and then having to play centre. Woods had the misfortune of having his appearances in the Ashes series restricted to that ill-fated 1979 tour and then against the 1982 Australian 'Invincibles' - playing at a time when our international team was at a very low ebb, whilst missing out on the vibrant home Test series against the Kiwis in 1985 and Kangaroos in 1986. For me, it's a shame (and an injustice) that John Woods doesn't get mentioned with the same reverence as the other great stand-offs like David Bolton, Alan Hardisty or Roger Millward. But he will always be a favourite son of Leigh, who have enjoyed numerous other fine international players, not least Mick Martyn and the inaugral World Cup winners Jimmy Ledgard and Frank Kitchen.

Men from the land down-under

(Above) **Kangaroos in 1959 perform their war-dance before the first Test against Great Britain at Swinton's Station Road. Leading the group is centre Harry Wells and you can see Rex Mossop directly behind him.**

THE chance to see an Australian touring team in action was always a highlight for Rugby League fans, in fact tours were one of the major foundation stones on which the game was built. That first sight of men who looked like sun-tanned giants, wearing the famous bottle green jerseys with the two deep gold vees across their chests, was a moment to savour every time the Kangaroos came to Europe.

I got my first view of those green and gold jerseys in 1959 when I saw the Australians play at Barrow. It was, in fact, only the second live Rugby League match I had ever been to when - on a late October Saturday afternoon in 1959 - Barrow beat the Aussies 12-9 in front of an 8,488 crowd at Craven Park. I can still remember a figure in blue scorching up the right wing to score the two tries which brought a Barrow victory - that was Frank Castle.

The 1959 Kangaroos made a massive impression on British followers of the game, as the growing medium of television was able to bring them to a much wider audience and they played a sparkling brand of fast-moving football. In addition, they launched a new superstar of the game who was to remain a hero for ever afterwards - his name was Reg Gasnier. Wearing his tour number seven, although a centre-threequarter, the young Gasnier became a Kangaroo at the end of his debut season in first-grade with his home club in Sydney, the mighty St.George.

(Above) **Reg Gasnier touches down for one of his hat-trick of tries for Australia in their first Test win over Great Britain at Swinton during the 1959 tour. That performance made Gasnier an instant hero.**

(Above) **Harry Wells on his way to a try as the 1959 tour began with a big victory for the Aussies over Leeds. *(Left)* Portrait of a Kangaroo tourist - captain of the 1959 team, Keith Barnes, smiles for the camera.**

Gasnier gained instant fame when he crossed for a hat-trick of tries in his first Ashes Test against Great Britain. That was in the opening Test in 1959 at Swinton and it came as quite a shock because, remember, the British team had outclassed the Aussies on their own soil during the 1958 tour. The Kangaroos of 1959 did not go on to win the Ashes, but they went mighty close. They lost the second Test at Headingley by a single point 11-10, after Brian Carlson (standing in for first choice kicker Keith Barnes who had a hamstring injury) hit the post with a goal shot. Great Britain managed to retain the Ashes by winning the third Test 18-12 at Wigan. This was one of the televised games, and it caused a big fuss because that kept the crowd down below the expected level at Central Park. Neil Fox kicked six goals for Great Britain, but the highlight of the match was a brilliant try set up by Gasnier for his winger Carlson. The 1959 Kangaroos, captained by Welsh born full-back Keith Barnes, were the last Australian team to lose the Ashes on British soil, but they layed the platform for their triumphs that were to follow.

Ken, Saints and the wonder try

(Above) **The Saints team all kitted out and ready for Wembley in 1961. Left to right:** *(Back row):* **Brian McGinn, Abe Terry, Bob Dagnall, Dick Huddart, Cliff Watson, Don Vines.** *(Front row):* **Tom Van Vollenhoven, Wilf Smith, Alex Murphy, Vince Karalius, Mick Sullivan, Austin Rhodes and Ken Large.**

(Above) **A painful moment for Ken Large at Wembley in 1961, but the Saints centre had the last laugh.**

WEMBLEY has seen some wonderfully memorable tries over the years, and one always mentioned when there's a discussion over the 'best ever' is the try scored by Tom Van Vollenhoven for St.Helens as they beat arch rivals Wigan in 1961. On a day when when London baked in scorching heat and a sun-drenched capacity crowd of 95,000 packed Wembley, I was a small boy watching the final on a tiny black and white television set among a group of farmers packed into a front parlour in the village of Nethertown, Cumberland. In a room hazy with pipe tobacco smoke, those farmers did not profess to be Rugby League experts, but they knew all about the star names like Alex Murphy and the local Cumbrian boy Dick Huddart. Best of all, thanks to the regular extensive coverage of the game in their daily newspapers, they were in awe of Van Vollenhoven and all expected the Springbok flyer to be the man to win the game at Wembley. That's when my father stepped in and, using his extensive knowledge of Rugby League, tipped them off that the man to watch was not Van Vollenhoven, but his centre Ken Large. And so it came to pass that Large proved him right, with his electric pace and ability to time a pass perfectly - all shown in creating the brilliant try which climaxed the 1961 Challenge Cup Final and made it safe for St.Helens. Large burst through, interpassed with the South African, and finally gave a perfectly timed pass which sent the winger round to the posts for one of Wembley's greatest tries.

Style of the Other Nationalities

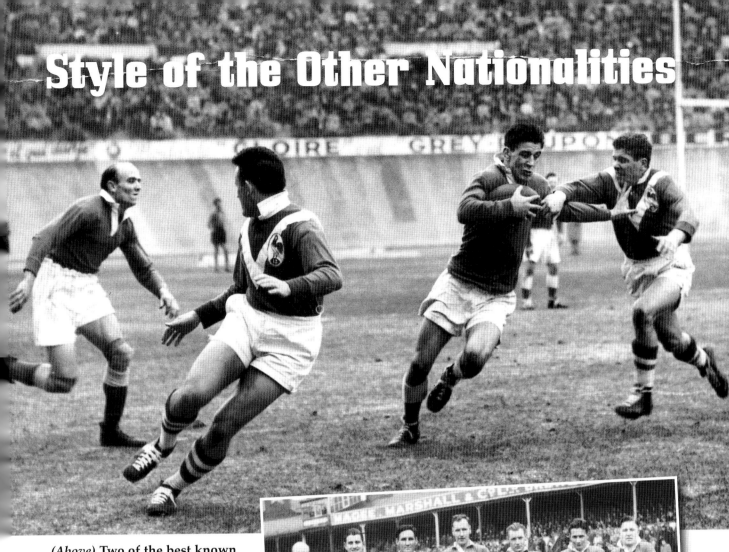

(Above) Two of the best known regular figures in the Other Nationalties team, Scotsman Dave Valentine (with the ball) and Australian Brian Bevan, in action against France at Marseille in 1952.
(Right) Other Nationalities before playing England at Wigan in April 1951 - left to right: (Back row): Bevan, Mudge, Daly, Robson, McKinney, Allan, Hunter.
(Front row): Devery, Bath, Cooper, Mountford, Valentine, Jackson and J. Milne (masseur).

THE Other Nationalities team of the early post-war years left an indelible impact on Rugby League, and still - over 60 years later - they are remembered with no little awe and admiration. It is remarkable that this team, clad in their green jerseys, have left such an impression on the history of the game when their era lasted, effectively , for only five seasons ... plus a last hurrah in 1955 when they combined with the remnants of the Welsh team to defeat both England and France and win the European Championship.

But between 1949-50 and 1953-54 the Other Nationalities were a massive draw and a big talking point in Rugby League as they brought together a galaxy of stars from Australia and New Zealand plus the occasional Irishman and Scotsman. It was one of the latter, Dave Valentine, who was almost a permanent fixture in the Other Nationalities line-up whilst, at the same time, being a Great Britain international. The magic of the team they called the 'Other Nats.' was that it allowed so many fine players from down-under to play representative football even though they were ruled out of playing for their home country in internationals. Most prominent of these was the great Brian Bevan, who never got the chance to play for his native Australia - and he was joined by other Aussie 'greats' like Harry Bath, Arthur Clues, Lionel Cooper, Pat Devery, and the Workington Town duo of Paskins and Mudge.

Hull F.C.'s league of gentlemen

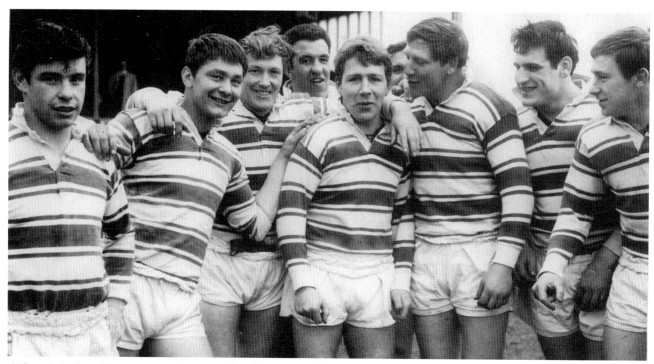

(Above) **Arthur Keegan was given a friendly reception by his Hull team-mates when he celebrated his testimonial with the club in 1969. Arthur was always regarded as one of the game's great gentlemen.**

HULL'S famous 'Threepenny Stand' at the Boulevard had a tough reputation for fans using the type of colourful language which would not be classed as gentlemanly - although most of it was good humoured. Yet among the players who were their heroes in the irregular black and white hoops were some of Rugby League's most respected gentlemen.

Although he played in a Hull pack which had a fearsome reputation, loose-forward Johnny Whiteley was always known as 'Gentleman John', and the game has had no finer sportsman. The same could be said of his great friend and full-back in Hull's successful side of the 1950s, Colin Hutton. After Colin had hung up his playing boots and moved to Hull K.R. as coach, a new full-back emerged at the Boulevard in the shape of Arthur Keegan. He travelled from his home in Dewsbury to Hull for every match and training session throughout his 13 years with the 'Airlie Birds', and was respected by colleagues and supporters as a gentleman. So well mannered was the young Arthur that he didn't argue when he arrived

(Above) **A reminder of how much the appearance of Rugby League players has changed - this well dressed group of young men were the Hull players in 1955 waiting for a train at Paragon Station before heading to Bradford to play Halifax in a Yorkshire Cup Final replay.**

at Headingley to make his debut for Hull against Leeds and was denied admission by the gateman who wouldn't believe he was a player. Arthur didn't want to make a fuss, so he went to the turnstiles and paid himself to get in.

Loiners got the Wembley luck

ANY lad growing up in Whitehaven soon became immersed (brainwashed?) into the local folklore about the 1957 Challenge Cup semi-final at Odsal Stadium in which Leeds were, according to everyone who was there and even more who weren't, very fortunate to win 10-9. So, in the eyes of most Cumbrians, the Loiners really were lucky to be at Wembley at all in 1957, and they rode that luck even more as they triumphed 9-7 over our north-west neighbours from Barrow.

Willie Horne and his men were back at Wembley just two years after their famous Cup win in 1955. The first controversy in Barrow's eyes came when Pat Quinn dived over for the Loiners' first try, but Barrow winger 'Gentleman' Jim Lewthwaite, widely known as one of the most honest men in the game, claimed that Quinn had lost control of the ball just short of the line. In the second-half, Don Robinson scored another try after Barrow's Jack Grundy passed the ball straight to him. Leeds had their name on the Cup!

(Pictured) One of the dramatic moments in the 1957 Cup Final as Leeds full-back Pat Quinn dives through the attempted tackle of his Barrow opposite number, Joe Ball, to score the Loiners' opening try. The Barrow winger Jim Lewthwaite claimed that Quinn had lost control of the ball just short of the line, whilst the Leeds hooker Bernard Prior (on the left) is anxious to say he didn't. The smaller picture appears to confirm that Quinn did just enough.

Honour of Salford's Red Devils

(Left) Historic memories of Salford's pioneering tour to France in 1934 which brought them their name of the Red Devils. This picture shows action from the second match of the tour, against Lyon-Villeurbanne on Saturday, 27th October 1934, which Salford won 34-17. On the right of the picture is the English referee Mr. A. Holbrook who had to stop the game several times to explain the rules to the French players.

(Above) Salford's 1969 Wembley squad on the top deck ready for an open-top bus procession through their city - players nearest the camera inlude: Colin Dixon, Bob Prosser, Chris Hesketh, Peter Smethurst, Ron Hill and Jackie Brennan.

The Red Devils won the Championship in 1973-74, a reward for the quality of the football they produced throughout the season.
(Above) The Salford captain Chris Hesketh receives the trophy along with David Watkins as chairman Brian Snape proudly looks on.
(Left) Watkins and the rest of the Red Devils in 1974.

ONE of Rugby League's greatest pieces of folklore surrounds Salford and how they got their iconic nickname of 'The Red Devils'. It happened back in 1934, as the code in France was kicking off its very first season and Salford undertook a pioneering tour to help the fledgling French clubs to promote the game. Salford played six matches between 21st October and 4th November, and arrived in Paris for the opening fixture to find themselves billed as 'Les Diables Rouges' - translated as 'The Red Devils'. They liked it so much they adopted it on their return to England and it has been their calling card ever since. Back in the 1930s at the time of the original Red Devils, Salford stood for quality with their attractive footballing team guided by manager Lance Todd and captain Gus Risman. And that was the inspiration behind the Salford Chairman Brian Snape in the late 1960s as he set about bringing success back to The Willows. Mr.Snape wanted the Red Devils to regain their reputation for swashbuckling open rugby and players with star quality, and his team proved to be the glamour side of the 1970s.

The shadow of York Minster

(Above) In this scene from Clarence Street in January 1958, York's Jackson tries to outpace Warrington's Jackie Edwards. York forwards in the background include Laurie Milner, Bill Hopper and Vic Yorke.

OF the many old Rugby League grounds which have now disappeared, the one I miss most is York's Clarence Street. Certainly the once great temples of the game like Central Park and Station Road are also big losses, along with the host of other famous old club grounds which are now no more. But there was a special affection for York - rivalled only by Blackpool's Borough Park.

It was, of course, all to do with its surroundings, just a short walk away from the historic city walls and in the shadow of the Minster. And the city of York, in addition to its obvious attractions, was a most hospitalable place for Rugby League fans because they could enjoy a match at Clarence Street and, within a few minutes, be back in the city centre where a host of well known former rugby players ran public houses.

In Rugby League magazines of the 1950s you could often see adverts, placed by Hunt's the brewers, inviting fans to *'When in York visit ...'* and then came a list of pubs with the familiar names of the licencees in bold type: Mel Rosser (ex-York, Leeds and Wales) at the Punch Bowl Inn; Jeff Moores (ex-York, Leeds, Queensland and Other Nationalities) at the Knavesmire Hotel; Reg Wheatley (ex-York and Leeds) at the Golden Lion. That was always

Jeff Stevenson

something very familiar in York and, no doubt, a big incentive when it came to recruiting top players to move to the Minster City - in later years, international stars like Tommy Harris and Dennis Goodwin continued the trend, whilst Jeff Stevenson was the landlord of The Fox and the Burton Stone. 'Stivvy' signed from Leeds in 1959 for a York club record transfer fee of £7,500 - it was also, at that time, a record fee paid by any Yorkshire club. Soon after moving to York he captained Great Britain to victory over Australia in the 1959 Test series - the last time we won the Ashes on home soil.

The Minster City was always an attractive place to play and several former Great Britain internationals took on the York coaching job at various times, among them: Malcolm Dixon, Alan Hardisty, Phil Lowe, Roger Millward and Gary Stephens. Sadly, the club said goodbye to Clarence Street in 1989 as more than a century of memories were bulldozed and it became a prime spot for housing development. Clarence Street had been their home since land was leased to the club in 1885 by York Lunatic Asylum. But in 1989, faced with the dilemma of having to spend £100,000 on ground improvements to keep it open, the York club sold it and left the city centre (and the Minster) for an out of town site at Monks Cross.

Hornets battled with big guns

(Above) Terry Fogerty playing for Rochdale Hornets at Oldham in 1974. Fogerty was one of several very experienced forwards who helped bring success to the Hornets at that time.

Doncaster met Keighley great at Bramley

(Right) Doncaster stand-off Eric Horsman on the attack against Bramley at the old Barley Mow ground in the early 1960s. The Bramley winger on the right is Terry Hollindrake, always remembered as one of Keighley's greatest players.

Classic style of Bradford's Ken Traill

(Left) The classic attacking style of loose-forward Ken Traill, pictured here in action for Bradford Northern against Dewsbury at Odsal in the early 1950s. A Lions tourist, Ken later was the coach of Wakefield Trinity's Cup-winning side of the early 'sixties.

The Batley-Dewsbury divide

LIKE all close neighbours in Rugby League there was always a healthy rivalry between Batley and Dewsbury, and derby games were often fiesty affairs helping to fuel the Christmas spirit. In what was known as the Heavy Woollen area, both Batley and Dewsbury had been at the cradle of the game as the Northern Union began to take shape in the late 19th Century. One piece of folklore learned at an early age was that Batley, with their wonderful nickname 'The Gallant Youths', had been the very first winners of the Challenge Cup, which was hard for young fans in the 'sixties to believe as now Batley were no longer among the top clubs. Going to both their grounds, Mount Pleasant and Crown Flatt, brought another surprise as both had very pronounced slopes. But Dewsbury made a comeback in the mid-1960s, twice going close in Cup semi-finals - and it would have been great to see those classic red, amber and black hoops at Wembley along with their mighty prop 'Tank' Walker - I often wondered how Eddie Waring, on t.v., would have been able to keep cool and maintain impartiality if they had got there.

Tank power

One player who crossed the Heavy Woollen divide very successfully, and was equally popular with both Batley and Dewsbury, was prop-forward Trevor Walker. They called him 'Tank' and never was a nickname more appropriate. After giving long service to Dewsbury, 'Tank' moved to Batley in the late 'sixties and made a massive impression - setting a new try scoring record for an open-side prop forward when he touched down 17 times in the 1969-70 season. (*Above*) Walker's power on the burst is shown playing for Batley against Leeds. And (*right*) the infamous moment in the 1966 Cup semi-final when 'Tank' met his match in St.Helens supporter Mrs. Minnie Cotton.

Gus and the Indomitables legend

IN the section of this book called 'Rugby League in the 'Forties' you can read details of the 1946 Lions tour and the team forever known in the game's history as the *Indomitables*. It was a part of Rugby League's folklore which every fan growing up in the 1950s and '60s knew about, not least because of the way it was recorded by Eddie Waring. These pictures provide another snapshot into that epic tour.

(Left) Captain Gus Risman, closely followed by Eric Batten, leads his team out at Carlaw Park in Auckland for the solitary 1946 Test match against the Kiwis. Despite being undefeated in the Ashes Tests in Australia, the British team lost 13-8 to New Zealand. As two of the most experienced players there was little doubt that, had the war not prevented a Lions tour in 1940 going ahead as scheduled, both Risman and Batten would have been in the team.

(Below, left) British players queue up for food during a meal-stop in their week long train journey across Australia, from Freemantle to Sydney.

(Below, right) Lions full-back Martin Ryan was an accomplished singer and journalist Eddie Waring, who proved to be a great publicist for the touring team, arranged for Ryan to perform a few of songs on the radio in Sydney.

(Left)
After disembarking from the aircraft carrier *HMS Indomitable* at Freemantle, the tourists had a wait of a week before they boarded a train to take them overland across Australia. Whilst in Perth, the British team played an exhibition match between themselves and this picture shows the leaders of the rival teams - tour captain Gus Risman and his vice-captain Tommy McCue, tossing the coin before kick-off watched by the match referee, a certain Eddie Waring.

(Above) Snapped outside the gates of the Sydney Cricket Ground after a victory - George Curran, Willie Horne, Jimmy Lewthwaite, Frank Whitcombe, Joe Egan, Albert Johnson and Tommy McCue with a friend.
(Above, right) Martin Ryan is helped from the field in the match at Newcastle after suffering a serious groin injury.
(Right) The crowning glory as the Ashes trophy is presented to manager Walter Popplewell in Sydney whilst other happy members of the *Indomitables* touring team look on.

Parkside the home of Hunslet

THE picture (*above*) has always been one of my favourite Rugby League photographs - not just for the classic action or the faces of the spectators in the crowd, but because it serves as a reminder of Hunslet at Parkside. For many years this picture adorned the front cover of Hunslet's programme 'The Parksider' - and it is a perfect illustration of the days when every club had its own unique appoach to programmes.

Parkside *was* Hunslet and this famous photograph actually is of Dennis Tate diving over to score against Batley on 8th September 1956. Tait was - like most Hunslet players - a local lad who came through the Hunslet Juniors before making his senior debut in August 1953. He went on to play 115 first team games for Hunslet, his last coming in January 1962 before he transferred to Bradford Northern - so that meant he found himself on the front cover of 'The Parksider' programme for many of the matches he took part in.

Dennis worked as a plasterer all his life except when that, and his rugby career, was interrupted by having to do his two years of National Service in the jungles of Malaya. Apparently he had just retured from Malaya when he played in that match against Batley in 1956 in which this never-to-be-forgotten photograph was taken.

Hunslet became, sadly, one of the clearest examples of the changing landscape in what were once the industrial power-houses of the north of England. And those changes had a marked effect of Rugby League. It remains a source of regret that one of the few 'old' grounds I never got to see a match on was Parkside (the other was Knotty Ash in Liverpool). The full story of Hunslet's departure from Parkside in 1973 has remained untold - the ground was sold to property developers and, after much heartache, Geoff Gunney rallied the troops enough to re-form as New Hunslet ... but no more at Parkside.

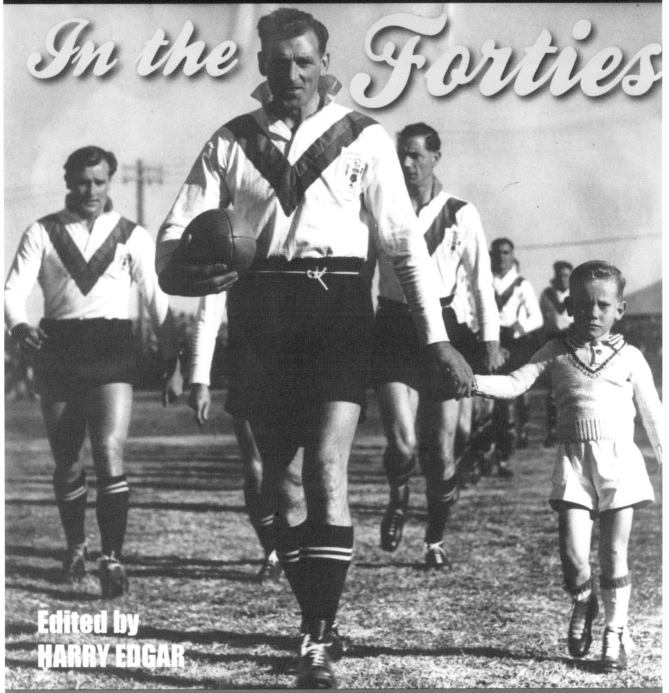

RUGBY LEAGUE

In the *Forties*

Edited by
HARRY EDGAR

Rugby League Journal History Series

Rugby League in the 'Forties

This section on Rugby League in the 'Forties continues the similar format of the previous volumes in our 'History' series in which we looked back on the 'fifites, 'sixties, 'seventies and 'eighties, including records of the Challenge Cup Finals, Championship Finals, County Cups, the major tours and the International Championship. Our aim is to ensure something is put down on paper, not just for our readers to enjoy right now, but for future generations to have the game's history recorded and presented to them in an easy to read and visually attractive version. With that in mind, you will notice that all publications from *'Rugby League Journal'* try to make full use of vivid pictures as we attempt to bring history to life, and for that we are always grateful for the wonderful images captured by the photographers of the day. Back in the 1940s there were none of the technological advantages enjoyed in today's digital age, but those cameramen on the Rugby League touchlines really produced some marvellous work, and we salute them.

Of course, the decade of the 'forties was overshadowed by World War Two. The first five years were the war years when all sports struggled to operate with any kind of normality. We have not covered the war years in great depth in this book, that might be something for another day, instead we have concentrated on the game's revival after peace returned in 1945 and Rugby League was able to engage in full competition again. But the impact of the war was never far away as the so-called 'boom' years began to unravel, and that was never more obvious than when the 1946 Lions touring team sailed to Australia on the air-craft carrier *HMS Indomitable* and then had to travel across that vast continent by troop train. That tour, and the legend of *The Indomitables* which should forever remain a landmark in the history of the game, is one of the pivotal events in the story of Rugby League in the 'Forties. It was quickly followed by the tours to Europe of the Kiwis in 1947-8 and Kangaroos in 1948-9; both were long trips in which the tourists were away from home for over six months, played before very large crowds, and both spent several weeks touring in a war ravaged France

(Above)
1947 action at The Willows as Salford's Harrison is chased by Bradford Northern defenders.

where the game was making a remarkable recovery from the terrible fate inflicted upon it by the Vichy government in 1941. The resurrection of the French game after that cruel war-time ban is a wonderfully dramatic story in itself, and it quickly produced a magnificent domestic competition in France featuring big city clubs, and played a key part in us having a vibrant annual International Championship in Europe in which strong French and Welsh

Birth of the International Board

teams were a match for England - an International Championship which was soon expanded to include an Other Nationalities team packed with the stars from down-under who had become such popular crowd pleasers among supporters of various clubs in the north of England.

The influence of those who had performed heroically during the war was never far away from Rugby League in the second half of the 1940s, not least the two off-the-field figures who played crucial roles in the game's rise to a position of such vibrancy and strength in Europe. In Britain, Bill Fallowfield, an R.A.F. pilot in the war, who became the new secretary of the RFL in 1946, and in France, Paul Barriere, a Resistance leader in the *Maquis*, who was the man who re-established Rugby League as an independent and recognised sport in his country and became the French League President whilst still in his twenties. Bill Fallowfield quickly had an influence on the direction of the game with his internationalist pro-European viewpoint and his commitment to the expansion of the game as a Welsh League was created, attempts were made to promote amateur clubs in London, two new professional clubs emerged in Cumberland and he tried to encourage other potential clubs elsewhere along with his unwavering support for the struggling Liverpool club. Fallowfield also was the prime mover in setting up the Rugby League Coaching Scheme in the late 1940s in which he enlisted the help of numerous experienced players, most notably Trevor Foster, another of *The Indomitables.*

For individual impact on the game in the 'Forties, on the field no man was more dominant than Gus Risman - during the war he won trophies as a guest player, mostly with Dewsbury, and made a massive impression in the Services (Rugby Union) internationals; he captained *The Indomitables,* and on his return embarked on a remarkable adventure in leading the new Workington Town club. Off the field, no-one could match the impact of Eddie Waring - his enterprise as manager of Dewsbury during the war brought great success to his home town club, briefly he was engaged by Leeds before travelling with the 1946 Lions to Australia when his journalistic career really took off. On his return from the tour Eddie was firmly established as Britain's best known reporter, he began presenting his film-shows which did so much good for the game, and was a campaigning columnist in '*Rugby League Review*' as supporters enjoyed a boom in the launch of new specialist publications - something you can also read about in the pages which follow.

(Above)
Delegates around the table at the inaugral meeting of the Rugby League International Board at Bordeaux in January 1948. Paul Barriere, who chaired this first meeting is at the centre of the group, whilst Bill Fallowfield, who took on the secretarial duties, is second from the right taking the minutes. Next to Fallowfield is the Australian Harry Sunderland, one of two journalists present at this historic first meeting - the other being Eddie Waring who can just be seen on the far left of the picture.

This meeting took place whilst the New Zealand team were on tour in France. The programme pictured at the top is from the second congress of the International Board, which took place a year later when the Australians were in France.

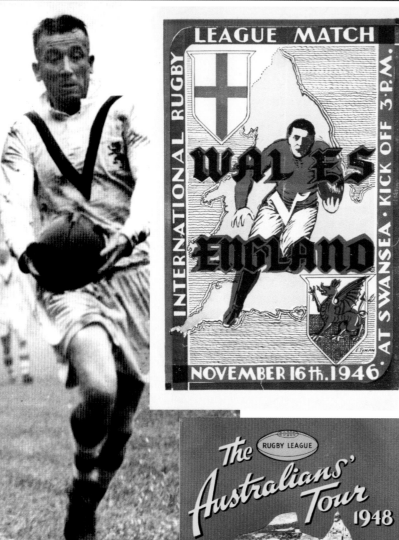

A taste of the colour of international Rugby League during the 1940s involving England, Wales, France, Australia and New Zealand.

Indomitables

SCRAPBOOK

The Rugby League News.

JOE JORGENSON
Aust Capt.

Gus RISMAN
Eng. Capt.

Official
Souvenir

Price
Sixpence

THIRD TEST
ENGLAND v AUSTRALIA
SYDNEY, JULY 20th 1946

Under the auspices of Australian Rugby League Board of Control.

BRITISH R.L.
AUSTRALIAN TOUR
1946

A souvenir of the Indomitables'
Ashes victory in 1946 - all the
autographs are genuine.

TIMELINE – THE WAR YEARS
1940-1945

The outbreak of war in September 1939 brought an immediate casualty for Rugby League with the abandonment of New Zealand's tour to Britain after just two games were played. However, in contrast to what happened during the first World War, the Rugby Football League resolved to continue competitive football and 'emergency' leagues were formed in Lancashire and Yorkshire, the winners of each playing off for the Championship. Indeed, during the summer of 1940 as RFL officials pondered whether to start a second wartime season, they were contacted by the Ministry of Labour expressing their desire that 'as much football as possible be played, so as to provide recreation and relaxation to the workers'. Several Rugby League club's grounds were requisitioned for a variety of purposes to help the war effort, and others had their capacities restricted because of the risk of air raids - notably Odsal Stadium which was initially limited to 15,000 spectators, although this was relaxed in time for some bigger crowds to attend Challenge Cup Finals there in 1941, '44 and '45. The Rugby League appointed an emergency committee to run the game and when they declared that match fees for the players should be set at ten shillings it prompted a strike by Halifax, Huddersfield and Bradford players. It was subsequently agreed that all players would received 25 shillings for a win and 15 shillings for a loss, and these rates continued (officially) until 1944.

A major feature of the wartime competitions was the presence of 'guest' players. Because military service and special munitions work meant many players were often unavailable to their usual clubs, permission was granted for players to guest with teams near their place of posting. One club who benefitted greatly from this 'guest' system was Dewsbury, who built up a powerful side during the war years thanks largely to the shrewd judgement and persuasive powers of their ambitious young manager Eddie Waring. Among the 'guests' Eddie managed to attract to Dewsbury were the great Welsh legends of the game, Jim Sullivan and Gus Risman, as both the Challenge Cup and Championship Trophy came to Crown Flatt.

Of course war prevented any opportunity of teams travelling overseas, so the scheduled 1940 Lions tour to Australasia did not take place. A match was played in May 1940 at Salford between the *'1940 Tour Probables'* and a team selected from the *'1936 Tourists'*. The 1940 'probables' won 29-21 even though their 1936 opponents included Gus Risman, who would have been a favourite to captain the 1940 Lions had the tour been able to go ahead. Domestic international matches between England and Wales were able to continue during the war years with six encounters taking place, one each year between 1939 and 1945 (inclusive), with proceeds being donated to war charities, usually the Red Cross. The England-Wales match at Oldham in November 1940 had to be stopped during the first half because of an air raid warning - the players were taken off the field until the all clear was given and the game resumed.

(Above)
Martin Hodgson, the great Test forward of pre-war years, who - on 13th April 1940, playing for Swinton at Rochdale - kicked a penalty goal from a distance of 77 and three-quarter yards - the longest goal kick (authenticated) in the history of the game.

(Left)
Dewsbury enjoyed much success during the war years, thanks largely to the shrewd management of Eddie Waring and his ability to attract numerous guest players. This Dewsbury team in the early 'forties shows manager Waring standing on the left, and includes such notable guests as the great Welsh trio Gus Risman, Roy Francis and Alan Edwards.

A positive gesture seen during the war years was the Rugby Union lifting its ban on Rugby League players appearing on the same fields as Union's 'amateurs' - at least for the duration of the war. As soon as the war was over, the Rugby Union reintroduced its blanket ban on those who had played Rugby League, but whilst hostilities raged players from both codes were free to mix in services football (although always under Rugby Union rules) and with the finest players from both codes playing side by side in services representative fixtures the standard of rugby was as good as anything ever seen in the 15-aside game. On 23rd January 1943, the two codes actually met each other on the field of play at Headingley when a crowd of around 8,000 saw the Northern Command Rugby League XV defeat the Northern Command Rugby Union XV 18-11 - under Rugby Union rules. A similar game was staged in April 1944 at Odsal Stadium when a Rugby League Combined Services team met their Rugby Union counterparts and, again, the League men won 15-10. The receipts from both games went to Services charities.

Rugby League lost one of its greatest personalities on 14th November 1942 when Lance Todd was killed in a road accident whilst on Home Guard duty. The successful former Salford manager and popular radio broadcaster had been a member of the pioneering New Zealand 'All Golds' touring team. In February 1943, at a meeting of Rugby League men in Manchester, it was proposed that a memorial trophy be introduced in Lance Todd's name - it was agreed to open a fund to be invested in Defence Bonds and use the interest each year to buy a trophy to be awarded to the outstanding player in the Challenge Cup Final.

(Above)
Lance Todd, one of the game's greatest personalities, lost his life in November 1942 in a road accident whilst on duty with the Home Guard.

(Left)
What a contrast for modern day Leeds fans to see such a sparse crowd at Headingley. This was a match between Leeds and Dewsbury in 1945. The Leeds player tackling an opponent is veteran Cumbrian prop Stan Satterthwaite, and other Loiners include Cliff Carter (no.9) and Reg Wheatley (no.10).

READ ALL ABOUT IT!

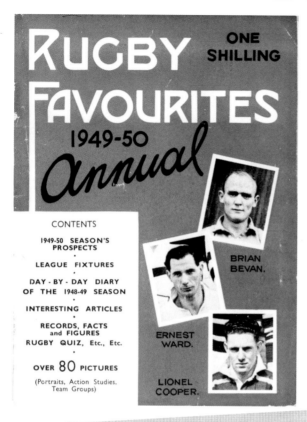

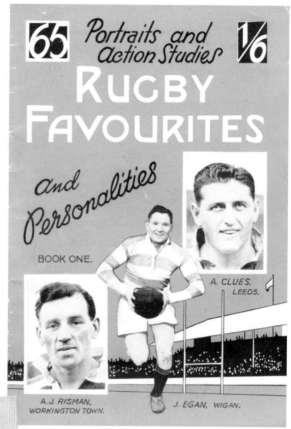

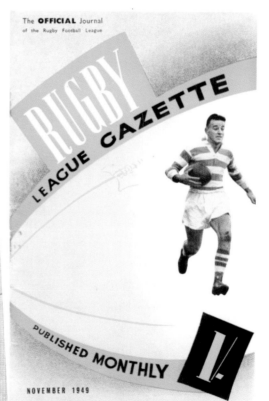

Some of the publications for fans to enjoy in the 1940s, including the very first issue of 'Rugby League Review'.

The rise of the printed word

It seems ironic that it was in the early post-war years of the 1940s, at a time when there were paper shortages and rationing, that Rugby League enjoyed an absolute smorgasbord in the creation of new publications. Maybe it was down to the massive post-war boom in public interest in the game which sparked a greater desire to read about it in more detail, or maybe it was just fate that a new breed of talented and creative individuals came along who wanted to produce publications and took Rugby League from its previous position of having no specialist title to the point, in the late 1940s, where it had several.

First among them was Stanley Chadwick of Huddersfield, who launched his 'Rugby League Review' as a monthly in September 1946. His first edition is pictured on the page opposite. In later years 'Rugby League Review' appeared fortnightly and eventually it became a weekly. Stanley was incredibly energetic and prolific, producing numerous other booklets - including one to celebrate the 50th anniversary Jubilee of Rugby League in 1945 - and, not content with getting 'Rugby League Review' out regularly his Venturers Press also introduced a pocket-sized quarterly called 'Rugby League Parade' in the 1947-48 season. Among the major writers who contributed to 'Rugby League Review' were the vastly experienced Tom Longworth and a young Eddie Waring, cutting his teeth as a fearless campaining journalist.

Following in the footsteps of the pioneering Stanley Chadwick, another far more modest monthly 'Rugby League Gazette' first appeared in 1947-48, published by 'Sports Reviews Ltd.' in Halifax. By the start of the 1949-50 season, 'Rugby League Gazette' had been adopted as the official journal of the Rugby Football League and with their financial backing it emerged as a more substantial, impeccably printed, magazine. It was obvious the RFL had become irritated by the outspoken criticisms expressed by Stanley Chadwick in 'Rugby League Review' and were eager to offer fans something that presented them in a more positive light. Among the 'Gazette's' regular correspondents was the same Tom Longworth, who had played a strong part in the early years of the 'Review'. In addition to these regular magazines, fans could also enjoy the fantastically illustrated booklets called 'Rugby Favourites' published by Provincial Sports Publications of Southport. They also issued an action packed pocket-sized 'Annual' at the start of the 1949-50 season - pictured on the page opposite. It was also at that time, on Thursday 11th August 1949, that the first issue of a weekly publication appeared - a four page newspaper called the 'Rugby Leaguer' published by Leo Stringman of Ashton-in-Makerfield. It soon established a regular readership and managed to outlive all the other publications, becoming a Rugby League institution.

(Pictured)
Clockwise from the top - the first edition of 'Rugby League Gazette' after its adoption as their official journal by the RFL in September 1949 - this one, rather appropriately, with a picture of their President, Lord Derby, on the front cover.
Issue number two of 'Rugby League Parade' in Spring, 1948.
And the second issue of the 'Rugby Leaguer' newspaper, published on 18th August 1949.

(Above)
The first published photo of the Rugby Football League's new secretary, Mr. Bill Fallowfield, as he took office in 1946.

(Above) **Willie Horne pictured practising his almost unique 'side foot' kicking style in 1946 whilst on tour with the British team in Australia. 1946 proved to be a good year for Willie as he starred for Lancashire as they clinched the first County Championship after the war and for England as they did likewise in the European International Championship. His Barrow team went within just one position of a Top-Four place and, of course, he became an *Indomitable*.**

(Above)
Jeff Bawden, who was the top points scorer in the Rugby League in the 1945-46 season with 239 - a feat he repeated in 1946-47 with 243 points. Jeff had become a Huddersfield player during the war in 1943, joining them from the Whitehaven amateur club Hensingham.

The first full season of competition after the end of World War Two, 1945-46, proved to be very eventful for Rugby League as the game got back into full swing again after the five dark years of conflict. The League had a new club as Workington Town were formed to bring professional competition to West Cumberland, but one their founder members, Leigh, were missing from the fixture list as they had been unable to find a ground after the war. The Northern Rugby League consisted of 27 clubs and the two County Cups were relaunched in their usual early-season format. International rugby was resumed in November 1945 as the first Rugby League game between Wales and England was played on the St.Helen's ground in Swansea in front of an incredible 30,000 crowd.

Around the same time club exchanges with France began again after Jean Galia had contacted the Rugby League in mid October eagerly seeking an English club prepared to go and help the revival of the game across the channel - Castleford doing the honours as they travelled by train to the far south west of France to play in Bayonne and Bordeaux. By 6th January 1946 Anglo-French competition was firmly back on the table as an 'English Rugby League X111' played a 'French X111' at the Parc des Princes in Paris, the English side (which included five Welshmen) winning 19-6. Soon after, on 23rd February 1946, full internationals for France were resumed as they played England at Swinton, going down 16-6. The biggest international event was the Lions tour of 1946, sailing aboard the aircraft carrier *HMS Indomitable* after the Australians, via their Minister for external Affairs, Dr. H. V. Evatt, wasted little time inviting the British Rugby League to send a team down-under. It was only whilst the tourists were in Australia that it was confirmed they would also travel on to play seven fixtures in New Zealand, including one Test.

(Above) The first Anglo-French international fixture after the war was in Paris on 6th January 1946. Here, loose-forward Ike Owens, of the 'English X111' breaks from the scrum supported by scrum-half Tommy McCue. They won that day 19-6 and both went on the 1946 *Indomitables* tour.

A major change in the administration of the game was seen from 1st June 1946 when the RFL appointed Flight Lieutenant (R.A.F.) William Fallowfield as their new secretary, in succession to the long-serving John Wilson who, as he approached his 70th birthday and with 26 year's service behind him, was retiring. 'Bill' Fallowfield was from a well known Rugby League family in Barrow-in-Furness and was chosen for the post of secretary from a list of 312 applicants, narrowed down to a shortlist of five with a set age limit of 45. On 19th November 1946 the RFL celebrated its 50th anniversary with a dinner held in Manchester. 1945 was actually fifty years on from the birth of the Northern Union in 1895 but due to post-war problems it had not been possible to organise a celebration function at that time. Despite making a healthy profit from the 1946 tour, the League turned down a request from the players for an extra bonus to compensate for losses caused by the tour's extraordinary circumstances.

(Above)
Jim Lewthwaite, the Barrow and Cumberland winger, pictured as one of the 1946 *Indomitables*. He was top try-scorer on the tour with 25 touchdowns in 15 games.

TOP TEN

1945-46

TRIES
35 E. Batten (Bradford Northern)
32 W. Best (Bradford N. & Leeds)
30 J. Taylor (Wigan)
29 E. Ashcroft (Wigan)
29 D. Baddeley (Wakefield Trinity)
28 J. Lewthwaite (Barrow)
28 G. Ratcliffe (Wigan)
27 R. Copley (Wakefield & Castleford)
27 A. Fiddes (Huddersfield)
26 L. Bratley (Wakefield Trinity)
26 C. Reynolds (Widnes)

GOALS
88 J. Ledgard (Dewsbury)
85 J. Bawden (Huddersfield)
76 W. Stott (Wakefield Trinity)
67 D. Clarkson (Hunslet)
63 J. Gibson (Bramley)
60 R. Rylance (Wakefield Trinity)
59 C. Knowles (York)
57 S. Powell (Broughton R. & St.Helens)
56 W. Horne (Barrow)
56 W. McWatt (Hull K.R.)

(Above) The Prime Minister, Mr. Clement Attlee, is introduced to the Wakefield Trinity team by their captain Billy Stott before the 1946 Challenge Cup Final at Wembley against Wigan.

(Right)
An illustration of the awful conditions as big freeze of 1947 began to thaw in March and Swinton entertained the French champions Carcassonne on a bog of a pitch heavy with mud. The *Canaris*, could not turn on their usual style and Swinton won 7-2

The post-war boom in attendances really took hold during the 1946-47 season with large crowds flocking to fill Rugby League grounds. However, the severe winter of early 1947 caused massive disruption to sport throughout the country as deep blizzards and the lowest temperatures recorded for many years left pitches unplayable and transport systems almost paralysed. After around two months of inactivity, Rugby League faced a huge backlog of fixtures so it was decided at the end of March 1947 that the season would be extended until at least mid June. In the event, the curtain did not come down until 21st June when the Championship Final was played at Maine Road between Wigan and Dewsbury. Playing so far into summer, and in the midst of the cricket season, badly affected the attendance, but there were no such problems for the 1947 Challenge Cup Final played at its usual time on the first Saturday in May, which produced a record crowd of 77,605 and receipts of £17,434. Such had been the demand earlier in the season that the Wembley Stadium officers had announced that the 1947 Cup Final would be an all-ticket match, the first time this had happened for a Rugby League game at Wembley.

The boom in attendances saw nineteen of the League's professional clubs declare a profit in 1946-47 and this new financial health, coupled with many club's willingness to pay big money to attract players from Australia and New Zealand, prompted local players to seek better terms. In January 1947 a new players' union was set up, led by the Leeds forward Chris Brereton, and by the end of the year

(Above)
In the international between France and Wales at Marseille in January 1947, French full-back Puig-Aubert tackles the Welsh centre Gareth Price as Trevor Foster looks on. France won 14-5 in front of 24,500.

they had achieved an agreement from the Rugby Football League on a new injury scheme for all clubs in which an injured player would receive £4 a week for 13 weeks and would then qualify for the Workmens' Compensation Act benefits. The RFL's management committee were also considering a scheme that would give a player a percentage of any transfer fee paid, that percentage to depend on length of service. But this was all small potatoes compared to the lucrative terms being offered to overseas players and those recruited from Rugby Union - for example, when Huddersfield announced the signing of Australian international Pat Devery in June 1947, he said his contract was a signing fee of £1,300 a year for three years, match terms of £7

(Left) Lionel Cooper wasted little time after his arrival at Huddersfield in becoming one of the game's top try scorers, and this picture shows a touchdown coming up against Leeds at Fartown. *(Below)* But when Cooper and fellow Aussie Johnny Hunter first stepped off the train at Huddersfield station they were met by the deep snows of the 1947 big freeze.

win, £6 draw and £5 loss, plus a return air ticket. Devery, along with Harry Bath who had signed for Barrow, was one of the players caught up in problems over being granted a clearance by the Australian Board of Control who were becoming very concerned over the loss of so many of their top players to English clubs. Eventually a five year ban on signing men from Australia was imposed on 7th August 1947, but not before such names as Lionel Cooper and Johnny Hunter (Huddersfield), Bruce Ryan and Duncan Jackson (Hull) and Ted Verrenkamp and Len Kenny (Leeds) slipped through the net. One Australian who had arrived without fanfare or any prior reputation, was a young winger called Brian Bevan who - after being turned down by Leeds - joined Warrington. The rest, as they say, was history, and at the end of the 1946-47 season Bevan was top of the try-scoring charts for the first time - the first of many.

With Leigh back in the fold and playing temporarily at the Leigh Harriers athletic ground, and the famous name of Broughton Rangers gone to be replaced by Belle Vue Rangers, the Northern Rugby League had 28 clubs in the 1946-47 campaign. Despite the backlog of fixtures stretching the season almost to the end of June, the New Zealand League were told to go ahead with their plans to come to Britain on tour in the autumn. Although the Australians had asked to be granted a tour in 1947, on the back of the highly successful 1946 Lions tour, the British Rugby League kept their promise to the Kiwis to welcome them at the first opportunity after the war. The tour proved to be a much needed success financially for the New Zealand League and also took them to France for the very first time.

(Above) Brian Bevan, the game's top try scorer for the first time in 1946-47.

TIMELINE
1948

(Right)
Action from two of 1948's most important matches. *(Above)* In the second Test versus the Australians at Swinton, in which Great Britain retained the Ashes with a 16-7 victory, forwards Dave Valentine and Bob Nicholson prove a handful for the Kangaroo defence. *(Below)* In the 1948 Challenge Cup Final, which drew a new record crowd of 91,465 to Wembley, the Wigan winger Gordon Ratcliffe is tackled by Bradford Northern's Alan Edwards as rival loose-forwards Bill Hudson and Ken Traill look on. Wigan won the Final, 8-3.

(Above)
Gerry Helme, scrum-half and key man in Warrington's team which won the Championship in 1948.

The Rugby League boom continued in 1948 as the Challenge Cup Final attendance reached new dizzy heights when 91,465 people were at Wembley to see Bradford Northern defend the trophy against Wigan. More prestige came as the Patron of the Rugby League, His Majesty King George V1, was the chief guest - it was the first time a reigning monarch had attended a Rugby League match and Wigan's Joe Egan had the honour of receiving the Cup from the King. Wigan were in the middle of a golden era in the early post-war period when, captained by Egan and coached by Jim Sullivan, they were present in numerous major finals and rarely far away from the top of the league. Built largely on local talent, not least Joe Egan, alongside such as Martin Ryan, Tommy Bradshaw, Ernie Ashcroft, Jack Hilton, Johnny Lawrenson, Gordon Ratcliffe, Ken Gee, and Billy Blan - all England internationals - Wigan also had two great talents from New Zealand in the shape of winger Brian Nordgren and stand-off Cec Mountford. This duo were two of the players in mind when the New Zealand Rugby League, like the Australians, eager to stop the flow of their best players to England, got the British Rugby League to agree to a ban on signing New Zealand players until the end of 1949, after which a £400 transfer fee would apply.

(Left) Great Britain captain Ernest Ward leads his team in training for the 1948 Ashes series. Next to Ward are Jim Ledgard, Stan McCormick, Russell Pepperell and Albert Pimblett, with Willie Horne and Johnny Lawrenson close behind them.

(Above) Ted Ward of Wigan was the top goal-kicker in the league in 1947-48 with a grand total of 141.

Bradford Northern rivalled Wigan as the most successful club of the time but, after losing at Wembley on 1st May 1948, they suffered a double disappointment the following Saturday when Warrington also beat them in the Championship Final. It was the Wire's first Championship in their history and, ably guided by coach Chris Brockbank, they played flowing football to beat Bradford 15-5 and bring first honours to Australians Brian Bevan and Harry Bath, alongside their budding English stars like Gerry Helme.

The Rugby Football League, now with their new secretary Bill Fallowfield firmly at the helm, were keen to expand the game to new areas. Doncaster, Mansfield and Whitehaven were proposed as likely places for new professional clubs and, eventually, it was at Whitehaven where these hopes became reality. This second West Cumberland club were accepted into the League at a meeting on 13th May 1948, but only by the narrow margin of 14 votes to 11. The new club appointed Bradford Northern's international centre Jack Kitching as their player-coach and kicked off in the 1948-49 season. The RFL were also encouraging plans to expand the game in Wales and London and - with so many grounds put out of bounds to the 13 aside game - there was talk of the League setting up an office in the capital with a view to trying to form junior clubs in the south east at industrial establishments with playing fields.

Early in 1948, as the Kiwis were wrapping up their tour in France, the first meeting of what was to become the International Board took place in Bordeaux. And the thirst for international football continued with little pause as the seventh Kangaroo touring team came to Europe in the early Autumn. The mother country had abandoned the term 'England' and played as the more inclusive Great Britain for the first time against the Kiwis in 1947, and so their victory over the Aussies in 1948 was the first Ashes series win under the name of Great Britain - which was fitting as the side included Welshmen and a Scotsman, as well as English.

TOP TEN

1947-48

TRIES

57 B. Bevan (Warrington)
49 G. Ratcliffe (Wigan)
37 L. Cooper (Huddersfield)
36 E. Batten (Bradford Northern)
36 A. Edwards (Bradford Northern)
32 J. Hilton (Wigan)
31 S. McCormick (Belle Vue Rangers)
28 J. Lawrenson (Wigan)
27 G. Aspinall (Salford)
26 J. Perry (Wakefield Trinity)

GOALS

141 E. H. Ward (Wigan)
102 J. Bawden (Huddersfield)
96 A . J. Risman (Workington Town)
89 F. Miller (Hull)
82 H. Palin (Warrington)
76 E. Ward (Bradford Northern)
71 E. C. Whitehead (Leeds)
65 J. Stott (St.Helens)
62 J. Mills (Keighley)
56 J. Ledgard (Dewsbury & Leigh)

(Right)
The 'babes' of Whitehaven joined the League in 1948 and the new club achieved their first major landmark of credibility on a Wednesday night in September 1949 when they beat the mighty Warrington 9-3. The 'Wirepullers' were giants of the game, with a side packed with internationals, and Champions of the Rugby League just a year before. This action picture from that game shows Whitehaven on the attack as international stars Gerry Helme, Bryn Knowelden, Bob Ryan, Harold Palin and Harry Bath lead Warrington's defence.

Bradford Northern set a new record by appearing in their third consecutive Wembley Final in 1949, in fact it was Northern's fifth Challenge Cup Final in six years and this time their captain Ernest Ward was able to lift the famous old trophy again after victory over their Yorkshire neighbours Halifax. A first ever capacity crowd of 95,050 established another new world record for the sport. The 1949 Cup Final was the first of many to be attended by Prince Philip, the Duke of Edinburgh.

That Wembley victory provided a much happier visit to the Empire Stadium for Ernest Ward than his previous one just two months earlier. On that occasion, under his captaincy, England had been beaten by France 12-5 in a European Championship match staged in London as part of the Rugby League's ongoing ambition to widen the game's audience to more parts of the country. Plenty of missionary work was going on around London and a Southern Amateur Rugby League was formed in 1949 with clubs at Brixton, Mitcham, Morden, Slough and as far away as Southampton. These brave amateurs faced much hostility, both from Rugby Union and their apologists in the London media - this, and the difficulty of finding grounds to play on - quickly put an end to this southern adventure.

Similar acitivity was going on in Wales and 1949 saw the birth of a Welsh Rugby League made up of eight teams: Aberavon, Amman Valley, Bridgend, Cardiff, Llanelli, Neath, Ystradgynlais and the Welsh Dragons (Cardiff). Later entrants were Blaina and Cardiff Rovers. To further encourage the game in Wales, at the end of the season in May 1949, the Huddersfield and St.Helens clubs embarked on a short tour playing each other at three different venues -

(Above)
Barrow's Willie Horne is unable to prevent a try for Wigan by Johnny Lawrenson at Central Park on 23rd April 1949.

Pontardulais, Bridgend and Abertillery - where crowds of 5,000, 10,000 and a remarkable 29,000 respectively gave an indication of the potential for the game in Wales at that time. Huddersfield travelled to south Wales as the newly crowned Champions of the Rugby League after their 13-12 victory over Warrington at Maine Road, Manchester on 14th May. A crowd of 75,194 set a new record for a game outside of Wembley, and they witnessed a magnificent encounter which was a fitting conclusion to a wonderful season for the game,

(*Above*) **Bradford Northern's Ken Traill sets the attack moving against Halifax in the 1949 Challenge Cup Final.**

and left most Rugby League followers wishing this kind of fare could have been served up at Wembley the previous week when a rather one sided Cup Final between Bradford and Halifax wasn't anywhere near as exciting. In the Championship Final, Huddersfield had led 13-nil, only for a thrilling rally by Warrington to pull the score back to 13-12 and set up a frenzied finish. That Championship Final had been preceded by a rather strange drama behind the scenes when the appointed referee, Mr. Frank Smith of Barrow, failed to turn up. His place was taken at the last minute by touch-judge Matt Coates and, fortunately, Paul Cowell - an experienced referee who was attending the match as a spectator - stepped in and ran the line in place of Mr.Coates. When an inquiry was made it was revealed Mr. Smith had not received the official notification of his appointment and it was presumed it had gone astray in the post.

With the new Whitehaven club settling in steadily, more expansion talk (albeit this time far less realistic) was heard early in 1949 when an application for membership of the League was received from the Glasgow Black Eagles. After close consideration, the application was deemed unsuitable and rejected by the Rugby League Council. Buoyed by their win over England at Wembley, France won the International Championship in 1948-49, and the competition in the following season was expanded by the inclusion of an Other Nationalities team. Packed with so many stars, they quickly wrote their own chapter in the folklore of the game. Also in 1949 a new transfer fee record was set when Warrington paid Widnes £4,600 for their centre Albert Naughton.

TOP TEN

1948-49

TRIES
- 60 **L. Cooper** (Huddersfield)
- 56 **B. Bevan** (Warrington)
- 36 **G. Ratcliffe** (Wigan)
- 25 **J. Hilton** (Wigan)
- 25 **J. Lawrenson** (Wigan)
- 25 **S. McCormick** (Belle Vue & St.Helens)
- 23 **A. Edwards** (Bradford Northern)
- 23 **J. Etty** (Batley)
- 23 **S. Llewellyn** (St.Helens)
- 23 **J. Wood** (Leigh)

GOALS
- 155 **E. H. Ward** (Wigan)
- 149 **H. Palin** (Warrington)
- 103 **J. Bawden** (Huddersfield)
- 76 **J. Jones** (Barrow)
- 69 **R. Morgan** (Swinton)
- 65 **A. J. Risman** (Workington Town)
- 63 **G. Langfield** (Castleford)
- 63 **E. Ward** (Bradford Northern)
- 61 **E. Davies** (Salford)
- 57 **C. Whitehead** (Bramley)

The Indomitables tour

(Above) The Indomitables - the 1946 Lions touring team pictured in Sydney.
Left to right: *(Back row)*: Ken Gee, George Curran, Les White, Bob Nicholson, Arthur Bassett, Joe Jones, Eric Batten. *(Middle row)*: Trevor Foster, Ted Ward, Ike Owens, Doug Phillips, Jack Kitching, Ernest Ward, Harry Murphy, Jim Lewthwaite. *(Front row)*: Martin Ryan, Albert Johnson, Tommy McCue, Mr. W. Popplewell (manager), Gus Risman (captain), Mr. W. Gabbatt (manager), Frank Whitcombe, Joe Egan, Fred Hughes. *(Seated in front)*: W.T.H.Davies, Bryn Knowelden, Dai Jenkins Willie Horne.

(Above)
Lions forward Trevor Foster in the opening game of the 1946 tour at Junee, in New South Wales.

The 1946 tour to Australia and New Zealand by the British team has a very special place in the history of Rugby League. The Lions of '46 will be forever known as *The Indomitables* - a fitting name for a team of such high quality sportsmen who overcame much adversity to perform at the highest level and write their name into the record books as the only British team to go through a three Test Ashes series in Australia undefeated.

This Lions team, captained by the immaculate Gus Risman, were a special breed of men who had just emerged from five years of war. Still billed as 'England' despite the presence of 11 Welshmen in the 26-man squad, the tourists got their enduring nickname because the only means of transport available to get them to Australia was aboard the aircraft carrier *HMS Indomitable*. They set sail from Plymouth on 3rd April 1946, and arrived at Freemantle 27 days later. An expected short stay in Western Australia turned into a wait of a full week as, with no ship available, a way of getting the British team across the vast continent was sought. Eventually, under Navy supervision, they got on

(*Above*) **Posing on the promenade at Newcastle, N.S.W. are Lions players Les White, Ken Gee, Joe Egan, Martin Ryan, George Curran, Jim Lewthwaite, Dai Jenkins, Ted Ward and Albert Johnson, along with the young journalist Eddie Waring and tour manager Wilf Gabbatt - that's Mr. Gabbatt's hat on the post!**

(*Above*) **Life on board the aircraft carrier *H.M.S. Indomitable* as Lions captain Gus Risman leads a training run with team-mates Albert Johnson, Les White, Fred Hughes, Harry Murphy, Ernest Ward and Jim Lewthwaite.**

board a troop train to undertake the 2,600 mile journey to Sydney - it took from 6th May to 13th May to travel from Freemantle to Sydney but, once there in the 'capital' of Rugby League, the Lions got down to business with the opening game played at Junee, New South Wales, against Southern Division on 22nd May. The tour proved to be a great success, setting new records for crowds and receipts - and Risman's men were undefeated in the Ashes series, winning two Tests to nil after and 8-all draw in the opening Test in Sydney.

The biggest man in the team, 19-stone Welsh prop Frank Whitcombe, made most appearances on the tour as he played in 19 out of a possible 27 games. His Bradford club mate Ernest Ward was leading scorer with 101 points, and the four wingers - Arthur Bassett, Jim Lewthwaite, Eric Batten and Albert Johnson touched down for no less than 76 tries between them. The 26 players were made up of six from Bradford, four from both Barrow and Wigan, two each from Leeds and Salford, and one each from Halifax, Workington, Warrington, Widnes, Wakefield, Huddersfield, Oldham and York. The 1946 team were the first to fly to New Zealand by sea-plane, and they realised a tour profit of £6,431 from which each player received a bonus of £123.

TOUR RECORD
First game: 22nd May 1946, at Junee.
Last game: 12th August 1946, at Auckland.
In Australia: Played 20, Won 16, Drew 1, Lost 3.
In New Zealand: Played 7, Won 5, Lost 2.
Total: Played 27, Won 21, Drew 1, Lost 5.
TEST RECORD
Gt.Britain and Australia drew 8-8. (*at Sydney*)
Gt.Britain beat Australia 14-5. (*at Brisbane*)
Gt.Britain beat Australia 20-7. (*at Sydney*)
N.Zealand beat Gt.Britain 13-8. (*at Auckland*)

The 1946 British Lions tour

In Australia

Opponents	Venue	Result	Score	Att.
Southern Division	Junee	Won	36-4	6,135
Canberra	Canberra	Won	45-12	5,095
New South Wales	Sydney	Won	14-10	51,364
South Coast Division	Wollongong	Lost	12-15	13,352
New South Wales	Sydney	Won	21-7	47,085
Western Division	Orange	Won	33-2	8,318
Newcastle	Newcastle	Lost	13-18	17,134
AUSTRALIA (1)	**Sydney**	**Drew**	**8-8**	**64,527**
Northern Division	Tamworth	Won	61-5	7,270
Queensland	Brisbane	Lost	24-25	21,500
Wide Bay	Bundaberg	Won	16-12	6,356
Central Queensland	Rockhampton	Won	35-12	7,070
North Queensland	Townsville	Won	55-16	7,567
Mackay	Mackay	Won	94-0	5,044
AUSTRALIA (2)	**Brisbane**	**Won**	**14-5**	**40,500**
Brisbane	Brisbane	Won	21-15	15,722
Ipswich	Ipswich	Won	29-12	5,237
Toowoomba	Towoomba	Won	34-5	9,863
North Coast Division	Grafton	Won	53-8	6,955
AUSTRALIA (3)	**Sydney**	**Won**	**20-7**	**35,294**

In New Zealand

South Island	Christchurch	Won	24-12	8,000
West Coast	Greymouth	Lost	8-17	4,000
Maoris	Wellington	Won	32-8	10,000
Auckland	Auckland	Won	9-7	20,000
South Auckland	Huntley	Won	42-12	3,000
NEW ZEALAND	**Auckland**	**Lost**	**8-13**	**11,000**
Auckland	Auckland	Won	22-9	12,400

New Zealand on tour 1947

(*Above*) **The Kiwis perform the 'haka' before their 1947 second Test victory over Great Britain at Swinton. It was New Zealand's first ever Test at Station Road, and they squared the series with an 10-7 win**

(*Above*) **Rival full-backs Warwick Clarke and Puig-Aubert pose for the camera before the first ever Test match between France and New Zealand in late December 1947.**

The 1947 New Zealand touring team played a crucial role in rebuilding the game in their country by ensuring it was restored to a sound financial footing after the disastrous loss on their 1939 tour which had to be cancelled after just two games following the outbreak of war. The British Rugby League honoured their promise to invite the Kiwis to tour again as soon as was feasible after the war, and bumper crowds ensured the New Zealand League gathered a healthy profit to clear their debts of 1939.

The 1947-48 tourists were the first Kiwis to play France, and they performed with great credit in the international arena - going within one point of a Test series win against Great Britain, beating Wales, and tying their two Test series in France. The Kiwis played 35 matches in an itinerary made all the more crowded by a delayed departure from Auckland because of a dockers' strike - the New Zealanders travelled on the *Rangtiki* which eventually reached London's Tilibury docks 17 days late. The delay meant the opening game at St.Helens was played just two days after arrival, and the first Test against Great Britain became the fourth game, only 11 days into the tour.

The Kiwis were captained by the Canterbury prop-forward Pat Smith, who led from the front by playing in 28 of the 35 games. Touring to a Europe still recovering from the ravages of war was a challenge well met by the New Zealanders, who carried ration books and were grateful for food parcels from home, which they often shared with the locals in the north of England. Although not up to full fitness by the time the first Test was played, the Kiwis earned much credit as they lost narrowly 11-10 to Great Britain. And New Zealand turned the tables by winning the second test 10-7 after a massive rear-guard action which overcame a huge scrum deficit of 74-16 at the hands

(Left) A nice moment before the Kiwis' tour match at Wigan on 22nd October 1947 as Cec Mountford was reunited with his brother Ken, a member of the touring party. Cec had forfeited a place in the New Zealand team when he left his native West Coast to join Wigan, and he went on to enjoy a long and successful career in the English game.

(Above) The New Zealand team pictured at Odsal Stadium before the third and deciding Test against Great Britain in 1947. Note, on the right of the group, former British captain Jim Brough, who acted as a coaching advisor for the tourists.

of Britain's master hooker Joe Egan. In the decider, the first Test to be played at Odsal, a big crowd of almost 43,000 saw Britain win in some style as the Kiwis continued to win friends. The tourists had already covered all their tour expenses after their game at Warrington on 15th November, and big crowds at their eight fixtures in France further added to the New Zealand Rugby League's profit. An additional unscheduled match was played at Antibes against a French military team, the game refereed by the Kiwis' co-manager Lance Hunter.

TOUR RECORD
First game: 25th September 1947, at St.Helens.
Last game: 25th January 1948, at Bordeaux.
In Britain: Played 27, Won 16, Drew 1, Lost 10.
In France: Played 8, Won 4, Drew 1, Lost 3.
Total: Played 35, Won 20, Drew 2, Lost 13.
TEST RECORD
Great Britain beat New Zealand 11-10. *(at Leeds)*
New Zealand beat Great Britain 10-7. *(at Swinton)*
Great Britain beat New Zealand 25-9. *(at Bradford)*
New Zealand beat France 11-7. *(at Parc des Princes, Paris)*
France beat New Zealand 25-7. *(at Bordeaux)*

1947-8 Kiwi tour

In Britain

	Result		Att.
St.Helens	Won	11-5	22,000
Swinton	Lost	6-8	12,148
York	Won	29-0	4,500
GT.BRITAIN (1)	**Lost**	**10-11**	**28,445**
Castleford	Won	17-3	11,000
Hull Kingston R.	Lost	7-13	12,000
Bradford Northern	Won	17-7	17,519
Leigh	Won	10-5	15,000
Wales (at Swansea)	Won	28-20	18,283
Wigan	Won	10-8	24,089
Oldham	Won	18-8	17,239
Hunslet	Lost	10-18	5,533
Hull	Lost	7-13	16,113
Batley	Lost	18-19	3,510
GT.BRITAIN (2)	**Won**	**10-7**	**29,031**
Leeds	Won	23-16	8,864
Warrington	Lost	5-7	20,682
Halifax	Won	21-5	5,276
Huddersfield	Lost	7-12	8,872
Widnes	Lost	0-7	11,900
Dewsbury	Won	24-5	7,270
Workington Town	Won	12-7	10,722
Barrow	Drew	2-2	5,565
Wakefield Trinity	Won	30-3	11,595
Bramley	Won	31-3	3,100
Belle Vue Rangers	Won	19-3	10,000
GT.BRITAIN (3)	**Lost**	**9-25**	**42,680**

In France

FRANCE (1)	**Won**	**11-7**	**12,000**
Catalans de France	Won	10-7	15,000
Languedoc/Pyrenees	Lost	0-15	18,000
Centre Lyonnais	Lost	10-20	12,000
Provence	Won	36-7	10,000
France 'B'	Won	41-20	25,000
Basques de France	Drew	3-3	12,000
FRANCE (2)	**Lost**	**7-25**	**22,000**

(plus -unofficial match at Antibes - Won 54-7)

Kangaroos on Tour - 1948

(*Above*) **A flick pass to Mel Meek in the opening game of the 1948 tour at Fartown.**

1948-9 Kangaroo tour

In Britain

	Result		Att.
Huddersfield	Lost	3-22	26,017
Belle Vue R.	Won	14-9	7,535
Hull	Won	13-3	16,616
Wakefield T.	Won	26-19	20,040
Leigh	Won	24-12	12,968
Salford	Won	13-2	16,627
Castleford	Won	10-8	14,004
GT.BRITAIN (1)	**Lost**	**23-21**	**36,529**
Cumberland	Lost	4-5	8,818
St.Helens	Lost	8-10	20,175
Dewsbury	Won	14-4	14,314
Hull Kingston R.	Lost	12-17	7,717
Wigan	Lost	11-16	28,554
Barrow	Won	11-5	13,143
Leeds	Won	15-2	13,542
Warrington	Lost	7-16	26,879
GT.BRITAIN (2)	**Lost**	**7-16**	**36,354**
Bradford N.	Won	21-7	13,287
Workington Town	Lost	7-10	13,253
Swinton	Won	21-0	5,849
Wales	Won	12-5	9,224
Yorkshire	Lost	2-5	5,310
Halifax	Won	10-8	8,850
Oldham	Won	21-7	14,798
Lancashire	Lost	8-13	11,788
Widnes	Won	18-8	10,761
GT.BRITAIN (3)	**Lost**	**9-23**	**42,000**

In France

Pyrenees Select.	Won	42-3	10,000
FRANCE (1)	**Won**	**29-10**	**18,000**
Catalans de France	Lost	5-20	15,000
Carcassonne	Won	13-8	8,500
Languedoc Select	Won	38-0	2,500
Cannes	Won	60-7	1,100
French X111	Won	30-8	4,000
Lyon/Roanne	Won	29-10	8,000
Cavaillon	Won	22-5	5,000
FRANCE (2)	**Won**	**10-0**	**24,000**

The tour of the 1948-49 Kangaroos was hit by a major controversy even before they left Australia when the incumbent captain-coach, Len Smith, was left out of the team. The unexplained non-selection of Smith has remained one of the most infamous mysteries in the history of Rugby League in Australia. His place as captain of the touring team went, instead, to Colin Maxell, a 30-year-old centre who had been dropped by his club Western Suburbs and could not win a place in the New South Wales team - leaving nobody more surprised at his selection than Maxwell himself.

The Kangaroos set sail for Europe on 4th August 1948 aboard the *Maloja.* As they docked at Marseille, time was running short before their scheduled opening fixture at Huddersfield on 18th September, so arrangements were made to fly the Australians from the south of France. Had they travelled on to England by sea as originally planned, they would have arrived too late for the game at Fartown. In the event, the cost of the flight was justified as a bumper 26,017 crowd paid receipts of £3,530 - which got the Aussies' tour bank balance off to a good start. On the field it wasn't such good news as a Huddersfield side including the Australian trio of Hunter, Devery and Cooper, beat the tourists 22-3 in a game marred by violent incidents.

In Australia, many people compared the 1948 Kangaroos to their pioneers of 1908 - as none of the 28 players in the 1948 side had toured before and, because of the war, it had been 11 long years since the last Kangaroo team had played on British soil. The shortage of food was a constant problem for the tourists in Britain. The players

(*Above*) **On a cold Wednesday afternoon, 24th November 1948, the Kangaroos' captain for the day, Wally O'Connell, introduces his players to Lord Derby at Headingley, Leeds before the tourists' 5-2 defeat by the Yorkshire county team.**

(Above) **The Australian team which toured Britain and France in 1948-49.**
Left to right: *(Back row):* B.Hopkins, F.Johnson, N.Mulligan, L.Cowie, E.Furness (trainer), D.McRitchie,
P.McMahon, W.Thompson, W.O'Connell. *(Second row):* J.Hawke, F. de Belin, L.Pegg, R.Dimond, J.Horrigan,
J.Rayner, J.Holland, N.Hand, K.Schubert, A.Gibbs. *(Front row):* E.Brosnan, D.Hall, W.Tyquin, Mr.
E.J.Simmonds (manager), C.Maxwell (captain), Mr. W.Buckley (manager), V.Bulgin, H.Benton, J.Graves.
(Seated in front): R.Lulham, C.Churchill, K.Froome.

were paid just £6 a week and were unable to obtain extra rations - but they had the compensation of sharing a very healthy bonus of £460 a man as tour profits reached £26,000, the 1948-49 Kangaroos drawing bigger crowds than any of their predecessors. Many of the Australian players enjoyed the French section of the tour much more than their time in the austere north of England, as the warmer climate and greater availability of food was much more like home for the Aussies. That showed on the field as the Kangaroos beat a strong French side in both Tests after losing the first two (and with them the Ashes) in England. The tourists returned to England after completing their 10 games in France to play the re-scheduled third Test against Great Britain at Bradford on 29th January. It had been postponed because of fog on its original date of 18th December - and, although it was a 'dead rubber', a bumper crowd of over 42,000 turned out. It was the end of a long road for a touring team that had been away from home for almost six months.

(Above) **The 1948 Aussies attack against Warrington at Wilderspool.**

TOUR RECORD
First game: 18th September 1948, at Huddersfield.
Last game: 29th January 1949, at Odsal, Bradford.
In Britain: Played 27, Won 15, Lost 12.
In France: Played 10, Won 9, Lost 1.
Total: Played 37, Won 24, Lost 13.
TEST RECORD
Great Britain beat Australia 23-21. *(at Leeds*
Great Britain beat Australia 16-7. *(at Swinton)*
Great Britain beat Australia 23-9. *(at Bradford)*
Australia beat France 29-10. *(at Marseille)*
Australia beat France 10-0. *(at Bordeaux)*

The Ashes Test series 1948

(Above)
Stan McCormick flies in at the corner for one of his two tries in Great Britain's 23-21 victory in the epic first Test in 1948 at Headingley. 12 tries were scored in a feast of flowing football.

Great Britain retained the Ashes against the 1948 Kangaroos, sending the Australians home with a three-nil defeat in the Test series. It was the tenth consecutive Ashes win for the British in the only series against the Aussies staged on home soil during the 'forties. Although Great Britain were to finish in total control, things had not looked so certain during the opening Test at Headingley which produced a remarkable, fast moving, clean game featuring 12 tries. In the closing moments full-back Clive Churchill was tackled inches short of a try which would have won the game for Australia. But that was as close as the Kangaroos got.

Great Britain had no coach in charge after Dai Rees, the Bradford Northern manager, turned down an invitation to coach the international team for the first Test. Rees said an appointment should be made for all three Tests, not just one, and Hunslet's Jack Walkington turned it down for the same reason, leaving the captain Ernest Ward to look after team tactics and organisation. The third Test at Odsal was postponed on 18th December when fog descended 40 minutes before kick-off time - it was played after the Aussies had completed their tour to France.

FIRST TEST
Saturday 9th October 1948, at Headingley, Leeds.
Great Britain 23, Australia 21.
Great Britain: Tries: Pimblett (2), McCormick (2), Foster (2), Valentine. Goal: Ward.
Australia: Tries: McMahon (2), Graves, Froome, Hall. Goals: Graves (3).
GREAT BRITAIN: J.Ledgard (Leigh); J.Lawrenson (Wigan), E.Ward (Bradford), A.Pimblett (Warrington), S.McCormick (Belle Vue Rangers); W.Horne (Barrow), G.Helme (Warrington); K.Gee (Wigan), J.Egan (Wigan), G.Curran (Salford), R.Nicholson (Huddersfield), T.Foster, D.Valentine (Huddersfield).
AUSTRALIA: C.Churchill; P.McMahon, D.McRitchie, J.Hawke, J.Graves; W.O'Connell, K.Froome; A.Gibbs, K.Schubert, J.Holland, D.Hall, J.Rayner, N.Mulligan.
Referee: Mr. A. S. Dobson (Pontefract).
Attendance: 36,529. Receipts: £8,020.

(Left)
The British full-back Martin Ryan finds himself surrounded by three Australian defenders during the second Test at Station Road, as Great Britain forwards Ken Gee and Trevor Foster keep a close eye on things. Britain wrapped up the Ashes in this game, winning 16-7. This game did not produce the same spectacular free-flowing rugby of the first Test, but the British side's overall superiority meant the result was rarely in doubt.

(Right)
Ernest Ward puts in a kick as the British backs stretched the Australian defence in the second Test at Swinton. Ward captained Great Britain in all three of the 1948 Tests as they held on to the Ashes. Trevor Foster is in close support.

SECOND TEST
Saturday 6th November 1948, at Station Road, Swinton.
Great Britain 16, Australia 7.
Great Britain: Tries: Lawrenson (2), Pimblett (2). Goals: Ward (2).
Australia: Try: Horrigan. Goals: Graves (2).
GREAT BRITAIN: M.Ryan (Wigan); J.Lawrenson (Wigan), E.Ward (Bradford), A.Pimblett (Warrington), S.McCormick (Belle Vue Rangers); R.Williams (Leeds), G.Helme (Warrington); K.Gee (Wigan), J.Egan (Wigan), G.Curran (Salford), R.Nicholson (Huddersfield), T.Foster (Bradford), D.Valentine (Huddersfield).
AUSTRALIA: C.Churchill; P.McMahon, J.Horrigan, C.Maxwell, J.Graves; W.O'Connell, W.H.Thompson; A.Gibbs, K.Schubert, N.Hand, N.Mulligan, J.Rayner, W.Tyquin.
Referee: Mr. G. S. Phillips (Widnes).
Attendance: 36,354. Receipts: £6,702.

THIRD TEST
Saturday 29th January 1949, at Odsal Stad., Bradford.
Great Britain 23, Australia 9.
Great Britain: Tries: Curran (2), Ward, McCormick, Williams. Goals: Ward (4).
Australia: Tries: Lulham, Mulligan, DeBelin.
GREAT BRITAIN: M.Ryan (Wigan), J.Lawrenson (Wigan), E.Ward (Bradford), A.Pimblett (Warrington), S.McCormick (St.Helens); R.Williams (Leeds), G.Helme (Warrington); K.Gee (Wigan), J.Egan (Wigan), G.Curran (Salford), J.Featherstone (Warrington), W.Hudson (Wigan), D.Valentine (Huddersfield).
AUSTRALIA: C.Churchill; P.McMahon, D.McRitchie, J.Hawke, R.Lulham; W.O'Connell, K.Froome; A.Gibbs, K.Schubert, D.Hall, N.Mulligan, F.DeBelin, W.Tyquin.
Referee: Mr. G. S. Phillips (Widnes).
Attendance: 42,000. Receipts: £6,875.

International Championship

(Above)
This classic photo shows French captain Robert Caillou streak into open spaces as Wales were beaten 19-7 at Bordeuax in March 1946. For many years after, a close-up of this picture of Caillou was used on the front of English programmes for international matches.

International Rugby League in Europe was at its peak in the years immediately after World War Two, and the annual championship between England, France and Wales drew big crowds and provided much excitement for players and spectators alike. The strength of both the French and the Welsh teams at that time, along with the public interest they generated in their own countries, were key ingredients in the success of the European International Championship - and they were very worthy rivals and respected opponents for every English team they came up against. The Championship quickly got underway again in the

(Below) Programme for the first visit of France after the War as they met England at Swinton in February 1946.

1945-46 European Championship

Saturday 24th November 1945, at St.Helen's, Swansea.
Wales 11, England 3.
Wales: Tries: Price (2), Owens. Goal: Risman.
England: Try: Nicholson.
Referee: Mr. G. S. Philips (Widnes).
Attendance: 30,000.

Saturday 23rd February 1946, at Station Road, Swinton.
England 16, France 6.
England: Tries: Johnson (3), White. Goals: Horne (2).
France: Goals: Comes (3).
Referee: Mr. A. S. Dobson (Pontefract).
Attendance: 20,000.

Sunday 24th March 1946, at Bordeaux.
France 19, Wales 7.
France: Tries: Dejean, Martin, Brunetaud.
Goals: Puig-Aubert (4), Comes.
Wales: Try: Foster. Goals: Ward, Foster.
Referee: Mr. P. Cowell (Warrington).
Attendance: 18,000.

Championship table:

	P	W	D	L	For	Ag.	Pts
England	2	1	0	1	19	17	2
France	2	1	0	1	25	23	2
Wales	2	1	0	1	18	22	2

first peace-time season of 1945-46, and a Welsh record crowd of 30,000 gathered in Swansea for the opening match against England. The strength of the two teams was illustrated by the fact that Wales included ten of the players who would go on to be *Indomitables* at the end of that season, while England had nine. France, under the astute captaincy of Robert Caillou, were quickly into their stride again after the years of war-time inactivity forced upon them by the cruel Vichy ban, and they shared one victory each with the other two nations in that first Championship. The following season, the tournament was expanded to both home and away fixtures.

(Above) **The Wales team which beat England 13-10 on 12th October 1946 at Swinton. Left to right:** *(Standing):* **W.T.H.Davies (Bradford), I.Owens (Leeds), R.Lloyd (Castleford), T.Griffiths (Hunslet), W.T.Davies (Huddersfield), D.V.Phillips (Oldham), G.Price (Leeds), D.Jenkins (Leeds).** *(Seated):* **F.Whitcombe (Bradford), M.Meek (Halifax), T.Foster (Bradford), D.Davies (Salford) and R.Francis (Barrow).**

1946-47 European Championship

Saturday 12th October 1946, at Station Road, Swinton.
England 10, Wales 13.
England: Tries: White, Dockar. *Goals:* Lawrenson (2).
Wales: Tries: Francis, W.Davies, Lloyd.
Goals: W.Davies (2).
Referee: Mr. R. Kendall (Keighley).
Attendance: 20,213.

Saturday 16th November 1946, at St.Helen's, Swansea.
Wales 5, England 19.
Wales: Try: Jenkins. *Goal:* W.Davies.
England: Tries: Johnson (3), Lawrenson (2).
Goals: Lawrenson (2).
Referee: Mr. P. Cowell (Warrington).
Attendance: 25,000.

Sunday 8th December 1946, at Bordeaux.
France 0, England 3.
England: Try: Ward.
Referee: M. Candeau (France).
Attendance: 24,100.

Saturday 18th January 1947, at Marseille.
France 14, Wales 5.
France: Tries: Joanblancq, Calixte. *Goals:* Puig-Aubert (4).
Wales: Try: Gwyther. *Goal:* W.Davies.
Referee: M. Candeau (France).
Attendance: 24,500.

Saturday 12th April 1947, at St.Helen's, Swansea.
Wales 17, France 15.
Wales: Tries: Walters, Harris, Williams.
Goals: W.Davies (4).
France: Tries: Maso, Lespes, Brousse.
Goals: Puig-Aubert (3).
Referee: Mr. G. S. Phillips (Widnes).
Attendance: 20,000.

Saturday 17th May 1947, at Headingley, Leeds.
England 5, France 2.
England: Try: Egan. *Goal:* Ward.
France: Goal: Puig-Aubert.
Referee: Mr. C. Appleton (Warrington).
Attendance: 21,000.

(Above) England winger Johnny Lawrenson on the attack against Wales.

Championship table:

	P	W	D	L	For	Ag.	Pts
England	4	3	0	1	37	20	6
Wales	4	2	0	2	40	58	4
France	4	1	0	3	31	30	2

International Championship

The closeness of the teams meant anyone could beat the other on any given day, but England's greater depth saw them retain the Championship in 1947-48. Action from their 20-15 win over France at Fartown *(below)* shows winger Albert Johnson tackling.

*(Above)*The England team before playing France at Fartown in October 1947. Left to right: *(Back row):* Mr. Guidicelli (referee), Alex Fiddes (coach), Ken Gee, Bryn Knowelden, Albert Johnson, Len Aston, Alex Dockar, Ernie Ashcroft, Eppie Gibson, Mr. Tom Brown (manager). *(Front row):* Eric Batten, Jimmy Ledgard, Les White, Joe Egan (captain), George Curran and Tommy Bradshaw.

1947-48 European Championship

Saturday 20th September 1947, at Central Park, Wigan.

England 8, Wales 10.

England: Tries: Ratcliffe, White. **Goal:** Rylance.
Wales: Tries: Thomas (2). **Goals:** Ward (2).
Referee: Mr. G. S. Phillips (Widnes).
Attendance: 27,000.

(Above) England prop George Curran versus France at Fartown.

Saturday 25th October 1947, at Fartown Huddersfield.

England 20, France 15.

England: Tries: Aston (2), Batten, Ashcroft.
Goals: Ledgard (4).
France: Tries: Trescazes (3). **Goals:** Puig-Aubert (3).
Referee: Mr. R. Guidicelli (France).
Attendance: 14,175.

Sunday 23rd November 1947, at Bordeaux.

France 29, Wales 21.

France: Tries: Dejean (2), Duffort, Lespes, Brousse.
Goals: Puig-Aubert (7).
Wales: Tries: Walters, Harris, Jones, Thomas, Goldswain. **Goals:** Ward (3).
Referee: Mr. A. S. Dobson (Pontefract).
Attendance: 26,000.

Saturday 6th December 1947, at St.Helen's, Swansea.

Wales 7, England 18.

Wales: Try: Foster. **Goals:** Ward (2).
England: Tries: Bowers (2), Ashcroft, Pepperell.
Goals: Horne (2), Palin.
Referee: Mr. P. Cowell (Warrington).
Attendance: 10,000.

Saturday 20th March 1948, at St.Helen's, Swansea.

Wales 12, France 20.

Wales: Tries: Price, Foster. **Goals:** Ward (3).
France: Tries: Lespes (2), Dejean, Beraud.
Goals: Barreteau (4).
Referee: Mr. Pascal (France).
Attendance: 6,500.

Sunday 11th April 1948, at Marseille.

France 10, England 25.

France: Tries: Barreteau, Calixte. **Goals:** Barreteau (2).
England: Tries: Batten (2), Ratcliffe, White, Clarkson.
Goals: Ward (5).
Referee: Mr. G. S. Phillips (Widnes).
Attendance: 32,000.

Championship table:

	P	W	D	L	For	Ag.	Pts
England	4	3	0	1	71	42	6
France	4	2	0	2	74	78	4
Wales	4	1	0	3	50	75	2

(Left) England stand-off Jack Fleming kicks ahead against France at Wembley in 1949, as forwards Featherstone, Curran, Nicholson and Joe Egan keep a close eye on things.

The pivotal match of the European Championship in the 1948-49 season came at Wembley Stadium where France managed to repeat their feat of ten years earlier by beating England on English soil. The fact that it was actually on the famous turf of Wembley made this victory all the more special for the French and they went on win the Championship by completing a double over Wales.

1948-49 European Championship

Wednesday 22nd September 1948, at Central Park, Wigan.
England 11. Wales 5.
England: Tries: Pimblett, McCormick, Helme.
Goal: Palin.
Wales: Try: Mahoney. Goal: Ward.
Referee: Mr. C. Appleton (Warrington).
Attendance: 12,638.

Saturday 23rd October 1948, at St.Helen's, Swansea.
Wales 9, France 12.
Wales: Try: Howes. Goals: Ward (3).
France: Tries: Taillantou, Perez. Goals: Puig-Aubert (3).
Referee: Mr. A. S. Dobson (Pontefract).
Attendance: 12,032.

Sunday 28th November 1948, at Bordeaux.
France 5, England 12.
France: Try: Lespes. Goal: Barreteau.
England: Tries: Pimblett, McCormick. Goals: Ward (3).
Referee: Mr. Guidicelli (France).
Attendance: 26,000.

Saturday 5th February 1949, at St.Helen's, Swansea.
Wales 14, England 10.
Wales: Tries: Daniels, Phillips. Goals: Ted Ward (3).
England: Tries: Lawrenson, McCormick.
Goals: Ernest Ward (2).
Referee: Mr. A. S. Dobson (Pontefract)
Attendance: 9,553.

Saturday 12th March 1949, at Wembley Stadium, London.
England 5, France 12.
England: Try: Ratcliffe. Goal: Ward.
France: Tries: Lespes, Calixte. Goals: Puig-Aubert (3).
Referee: Mr. A. S. Dobson (Pontefract).
Attendance: 12,382.

Sunday 10th April 1949, at Marseille.
France 11, Wales 0.
France: Tries: Cantoni (2), Lespes. Goal: Puig-Aubert.
Referee: Mr. Martung (France).
Attendance: 30,000.

Championship table:

	P	W	D	L	For	Ag.	Pts
France	4	3	0	1	40	26	6
England	4	2	0	2	38	36	4
Wales	4	1	0	3	28	44	2

(Left) England's Stan McCormick brought down by French winger Ode Lespes at Wembley in 1949 as full-back Puig-Aubert looks on.

(Above)
In the debut match of Other Nationalities, centre Tony Paskins sends out a pass to his wingman Brian Bevan against England at Workington. Three of the English defenders in the picture are Cumbrians: Billy Ivison, Jimmy Hayton and George Clark, with Barrow's Willie Horne closest to Paskins.

The International Championship gained a fourth participant, and a whole new dimension, with the arrival of the Other Nationalities team in the 1949-50 season. This meant the four nations played each other just once in a tournament interspersed throughout the season, with the first match on 19th September and the last on 1st March. The launch of the Other Nationalities had its roots in a short tour to France at the end of the previous season by a selection dubbed the 'British Empire' - who played a full strength French side at Bordeaux and were beaten 23-10.

Other Nationalities made their formal debut in the opening match of the 1949-50 Championship against England on a Monday evening in September at Workington's Borough Park ground, where a crowd of 17,576 turned out to welcome the international game. They had plenty of local interest with Workington Town's Lawrenson, Hayton and Ivison in the England team, plus Aussie favourites Tony Paskins and Johnny Mudge with the 'visitors'. This first Other Nationalities line-up consisted of ten Australians, two Scotsmen and a South African. Their team was: G.Wilson (Huddersfield); B.Bevan (Warrington), A.Paskins (Workington), R.Bartlett (Leeds), L.Cooper (Huddersfield)); P.Devery (Huddersfield), D.Jackson (Hull); R.McMaster (Leeds), K.Kearney (Leeds), J.Pansegrouw (Halifax), H.Bath (Warrington), J.Mudge (Workington) and D.Valentine (Huddersfield). It was a side good enough to beat England 13-7 on the night and the Other Nationalities became a colourful and popular part of the annual Championship, sharing top spot with England in their first season after beating Wales at Abertillery but losing away to France.

(Left) **England captain Ernest Ward attempts to tackle French centre Paul Dejean in the match at Wembley, won 12-5 by France, in March 1949.**

(*Above*) Wales and France line up at the St.Helen's ground in Swansea on 12th November 1949, before a match won by the Welsh 16-8. The Welsh players lined up as they were numbered on the field, from the left: R.Morgan (Swinton), A.Daniels (Halifax), J.Mahoney (Dewsbury), L.Williams (Hunslet), D.Boocker (Wakefield), J.Davies (Salford), W.G.Morgan (Cardiff), T.Danter (Hull), F.Osmond (Swinton), E.Hawkins (Salford), E.Gwyther (Belle Vue Rangers), W.J.D.Howes (Wakefield) and Bryn Goldswain (Oldham).

1949-50 European Championship

Monday 19th Sept. 1949, at Borough Park, Workington.
England 7, Other Nationalities 13.
England: Try: Clark. *Goals:* Ledgard (2).
Other Nationalities: Tries: Bevan (2), Wilson.
Goals: Devery, Bath.
Referee: Mr. C. Appleton (Warrington).
Attendance: 17,576.

Saturday 22nd October 1949, at Abertillery.
Wales 5, Other Nationalities 6.
Wales: Try: Davies. *Goal:* Davies.
Other Nationalities: Tries: Bevan, Cooper.
Referee: Mr. C. Appleton (Warrington).
Attendance: 2,000.

Saturday 12th November 1949, at St.Helen's, Swansea.
Wales 16, France 8.
Wales: Tries: Daniels, Williams, W.G. Morgan, Gwyther. *Goals:* R.Morgan (2).
France: Tries: Lespes, Contrastin. *Goal:* Puig-Aubert.
Referee: Mr. A. S. Dobson (Pontefract).
Attendance: 4,749.

Sunday 4th December 1949, at Bordeaux.
France 5, England 13.
France: Try: Cantoni. *Goal:* Puig-Aubert.
England: Tries: Ryan, Hilton, Gee. *Goals:* Ward (2).
Referee: Mr. Martung (France).
Attendance: 20,598.

Sunday 15th January 1950, at Marseille.
France 8, Other Nationalities 3.
France: Tries: Contrastin (2).
Goal: Dejean.
Other Nationalities: Try: Bartlett.
Referee: Mr. Guidicelli (France).
Attendance: 20,000.

Wednesday 1st March 1950, at Central Park, Wigan.
England 11, Wales 6.
England: Tries: Hilton (3).
Goal: Ward.
Wales: Tries: Daniels, Williams.
Referee: Mr. C. Appleton (Warrington).
Attendance: 27,500.

(*Above*) Jean Galia, pioneer of the game in France, pictured shortly before his sudden death on 17th January 1949. In his memory, the European Champions from 1949-50 onwards were awarded the Jean Galia trophy.

Championship table:

	P	W	D	L	For	Ag.	Pts
England	3	2	0	1	31	24	4
Other Nats.	3	2	0	2	22	20	4
Wales	3	1	0	2	27	25	2
France	3	1	0	2	21	32	2

Challenge Cup Finals

(Above)
Wakefield Trinity enjoy victory in the first post-war Cup Final back at Wembley in 1946, with captain Billy Stott holding the trophy. His late goal was the match winner.

The Challenge Cup was suspended after war was declared in September 1939, but the Rugby League were able to revive their most prestigious competition in the 1940-41 season. During the war years clubs were allowed to play 'guest' players and, after two Finals at Odsal Stadium both won by Leeds against Halifax, a two-leg system was employed with Dewsbury, Bradford and Huddersfield emerging triumphant. With the war over, the game was able to return to Wembley in 1946 when Wakefield beat favourites Wigan and Billy Stott became the very first winner of the new Lance Todd Memorial Trophy as man-of-the-match.

Challenge Cup Finals in the 'Forties

1941
Saturday 17h May 1941, at Odsal Stadium, Bradford.
Leeds 19, Halifax 2.
Leeds: Tries: Hey (2), Lawrenson (2), Jenkins.
Goals: Eaton (2). *Halifax: Goal:* Meek.
LEEDS: C.Eaton; E.Batten*, C.Evans, V.Hey, J.Lawrenson*; O.Morris, D.Jenkins; D.Prosser, C.Murphy, E.Bennett*, S.Satterthwaite, B.Pearson*, E.Tattersfield.
HALIFAX: A.Bassett; J.Bevan, C.Smith, F.Rule, A.E.Doyle; G.Todd, T.McCue*; F.Osborne*, M.Meek, H.Irving, H.Millington*, C.Brereton, H.Beverley.
Referee: Mr. P. Cowell (Warrington).
Attendance: 28,500. Receipts: £1,703.
Guest players: Leeds: Batten and Bennett (Hunslet), Lawrenson (Wigan), Pearson (Bramley). *Halifax:* Osborne (Salford), McCue and Millington (Widnes).

1942
Saturday, 6th June 1942, at Odsal Stadium, Bradford.
Leeds 15, Halifax 10.
Leeds: Tries: Edwards (2), Morris.
Goals: Risman (3).
Halifax: Goals: Lockwood (5).
LEEDS: J.Brough; A.Edwards*, A.J.Risman*, V.Hey, C.Evans; O.Morris, D.Jenkins; D.Prosser, C.Murphy, S.Satterthwaite, F.Gregory*, G.Brown*, E.Tattersfield.
HALIFAX: H.Lockwood; J.Bevan, C.Smith, F.Rule, A.E.Doyle; G.Todd, T.McCue*; C.Brereton, C.Jones*, H.Irving, H.Millington*, M.Meek, J.Dixon.
Referee: Mr. P. Cowell (Warrington).
Attendance: 15,250. Receipts: £1,276.
* Guest players: *Leeds:* Edwards and Risman (Salford), Grgeory (Warrington), Brown (Batley). *Halifax:* McCue, Jones and Millington (Widnes).

Stott's late penalty gave Trinity a 13-12 win after Wigan, with Martin Ryan and Ted Ward travelling with the *Indomitables* to Australia, were unable to convert any of their four tries. For the rest of the decade, Bradford Northern became synonymous with Wembley, setting a new record of playing in three consecutive Finals beneath the twin towers. Bradford, captained by Ernest Ward, coached by Dai Rees, and with Welshman Trevor Foster in his pomp, were a dominant force in the game in this era.

(Above, left): **Bradford winger Eric Batten kicks ahead against Wigan in the 1944 war-time Cup Final second leg at Odsal. Bradford won on aggregate, but Wigan got their revenge in 1948** *(above, right)* **as Joe Egan captained them to an 8-3 victory over Northern at Wembley.**

1943
Dewsbury beat Leeds 16-15 on aggregate.
First leg - Saturday 24th April 1943.
Dewsbury 16, Leeds 9.
Dewsbury: Tries: Edwards, Robinson, Kenny, Seeling.
Goals: Seeling (2).
Leeds: Try: Eaton. Goals: Eaton (3).
DEWSBURY: G.Bunter*; B.Hudson*, A.Edwards*, J.Robinson*, R.Lloyd*; T.Kenny*, H.Royal; H.Hammond, G.Curran*, J.Gardner*, G.Kershaw, F.Smith, C.Seeling.
LEEDS: J.Walkington*; C.Eaton, S.Rookes*, D.Warrior, C.Callaghan; C.Evans, D.Jenkins; D.Prosser, C.Murphy, S.Satterthwaite, K.Jubb, F.Gregory*, E.Tattersfield.
Referee: Mr. G. S. Phillips (Widnes).
Attendance: 10,470. Receipts: £823.
*Guest players: Dewsbury: Bunter (Broughton Rangers), Hudson, Edwards, Kenny, Curran and Gardner (Salford), Robinson and Lloyd (Castleford). Leeds: Walkington and Rookes (Hunslet), Gregory (Warrington).

Second leg - Monday 26th April 1943.
Leeds 6, Dewsbury 0.
Leeds: Goals: Walkington, Eaton, Jenkins.
LEEDS: J.Walkington*; E.Batten*, D.Warrior, C.Eaton, C.Callaghan; C.Evans, D.Jenkins; D.Prosser, C.Murphy, S.Satterthwaite, K.Jubb, F.Gregory*, E.Tattersfield.
DEWSBURY: G.Bunter*; B.Hudson*, A.Edwards*, J.Robinson*, R.Lloyd*; T.Kenny*, H.Royal; H.Hammond, G.Curran*, J.Gardner*, G.Kershaw, F.Smith, C.Seeling.
Referee: Mr. G. S. Phillips (Widnes).
Attendance: 16,000. Receipts: £1,521.
*Guest players: Leeds: Walkington and Batten (Hunslet), Gregory (Warrington). Dewsbury: Bunter (Broughton R., Hudson, Edwards, Kenny, Curran and Gardner (Salford), Robinson and Lloyd (Castleford).

1944
Bradford N. beat Wigan 8-3 on aggregate.
First leg - Saturday 15th April 1944.
Wigan 3, Bradford Northern 0.
Wigan: Try: Featherstone.
WIGAN: J.Sullivan; J.Lawrenson, W.Belshaw*, J.Maloney*, E.Ashcroft; M.Ryan, H.Gee; K.Gee, J.Egan, J.Blan, J.Featherstone, E.Watkins, J.Bowen.
BRADFORD N.: G.Carmichael; E.Batten, G.Bennett, E.Ward, W.Best; W.T.H.Davies, D.Ward; F.Whitcombe, V.Darlison, L.Higson, L.Roberts, W.Hutchinson, A.Marklew*.
Referee: Mr. S. Adams (Hull).
Attendance: 21,500.
Receipts: £1,663.
* Guest players: Wigan: Belshaw (Warrington), Maloney (Liverpool Stanley). Bradford Northern: Marklew (Barrow).

Tommy Bradshaw - at Wembley in 1946 and 1948.

Second leg - Saturday 22nd April 1944.
Bradford Northern 8, Wigan 0.
Bradford N.: Tries: Batten, Whitcombe.
Goal: Carmichael.
BRADFORD N.: G.Carmichael; E.Batten, J.Kitching, E.Ward, E.Walters; G.Bennett, D.Ward; F.Whitcombe, V.Darlison, L.Higson, T.Foster, L.Roberts, W.Hutchinson.
WIGAN: J.Jones; J.Lawrenson, W.Belshaw*, J.Maloney*, E.Ashcroft; M.Ryan, H.Gee; K.Gee, J.Egan, J.Blan, J.Featherstone, E.Watkins, J.Bowen.
Referee: Mr. P. Cowell (Warrington).
Attendance: 30,000. Receipts: £2,061.
*Guest players: Wigan: Belshaw (Warrington), Maloney (Liverpool Stanley).

(Above) Bradford Northern became the first club to achieve the distinction of going to Wembley three years in succession - winning in 1947 against Leeds and 1949 against Halifax, with a defeat by Wigan sandwiched in-between in 1948. They were captained on all three occasions by international centre by Ernest Ward, and this picture shows him with his victorious team after their 1947 Cup Final win over Leeds. Skipper Ward is held aloft on the shoulders of hooker Vic Darlison and centre Jack Kitching.

1945

Huddersfield beat Bradford 13-9 on agg.

First leg - Saturday 28th April 1945.

Huddersfield 7, Bradford Northern 4.

Huddersfield: Try: Peake. Goals: Bawden (2).
Bradford Northern: Goals: E.Ward (2).
HUDDERSFIELD: W.Leake; O.Peake*, A.Fiddes, R.D.Lewis*, J.Bawden; T.L.Grahame, A.Pepperell; J.Bradbury*, H.Whitehead, J.Miller*, K.Mallinson, L.Baxter, A.Givvons.
BRADFORD N.: E.Ward; E.Batten, A.Edwards*, J.Kitching, W.Best; G.Bennett, D.Ward; F.Whitcombe, V.Darlison, L.Higson, L.Roberts, A.Marklew*, W.Hutchinson.
Referee: Mr. F. Fairhurst (Wigan).
Attendance: 9,041. Receipts: £1,184.
*Guest players: Huddersfield: Peake and Miller (Warrington), Lewis (Swinton), Bradbury (Salford). Bradford Northern: Edwards (Salford), Marklew (Barrow)

Second leg - Saturday 5th May 1945.

Bradford Northern 5, Huddersfield 6.

Bradford Northern: Try: Batten.
Goal: E.Ward.
Huddersfield: Tries: Bawden (2).
BRADFORD N.: E.Ward; E.Batten, A.Edwards*, J.Kitching, W.Best; W.T.H.Davies, D.Ward; F.Whitcombe, V.Darlison, L.Higson, L.Roberts, H.Smith, W.Hutchinson.
HUDDERSFIELD: W.Leake; O.Peake*, A.,Fiddes, R.D.Lewis*, J.Bawden; T.L.Grahame, A.Pepperell; K.Mallinson, H.Whitehead, J.Miller*, A.Givvons, J.Aspinall, L.Baxter.
Referee: Mr. G. S. Phillips (Widnes).
Attendance: 17,500. Receipts: £2,050.
*Guest players: Bradford Northern: Edwards (Salford). Huddersfield: Peake and Miller (Warrington), Lewis (Swinton).

(Above) Wigan's Joe Egan became the first Rugby League club captain to receive the Cup from a reigning monarch in 1948 as he had the honour of being greeted by King George V1 at Wembley. A new world record crowd of 91,465 had witnessed Wigan's 8-3 victory over Bradford Northern - a defeat that could not prevent Northern's giant prop Frank Whitcombe being chosen as the Lance Todd Trophy winner. *(Right)* 1947 action at Wembley as the Leeds defence struggles to halt a Bradford attack as Australian forward Arthur Clues looks on.

1946

Saturday 4th May 1946, at Wembley Stadium
Wakefield Trinity 13, Wigan 12.
Wakefield: Tries: Stott (2), Croston.
Goals: Stott (2).
Wigan: Tries: Nordgren (2), Jolley, J.Blan.
WAKEFIELD: W.Teall; R.Rylance, W.Stott, J.Croston, D.Baddeley; J.Jones, H.Goodfellow; H.Wilkinson, L.Marston, J.Higgins, H.Exley, W.L.D.Howes, L.Bratley.
WIGAN: J.Cunliffe; B.Nordgren, G.Ratcliffe, E.Ashcroft, G.Jolley; R.Lowrey, T.Bradshaw; G.Banks, J.Blan, F.Barton, E.Watkins, H.Atkinson, W.Blan.
Referee: Mr. A. Hill (Leeds)
Attendance: 54,730. Receipts: £12,013.

1947

Saturday 3rd May 1947, at Wembley Stadium
Bradford Northern 8, Leeds 4.
Bradford: Tries: Walters, Foster.
Goal: E.Ward.
Leeds: Goals: Cook (2).
BRADFORD: G.Carmichael; E.Batten, J.Kitching, E.Wrad, E.Walters; W.T.H.Davies, D.Ward; F.Whitcombe, V.Darlison, H.Smith, B.Tyler, T.Foster, H.Evans.
LEEDS: B.Cook; T.Cornelius, G.Price, T.L.Williams, E.Whitehead; R.Williams, D.Jenkins; C.Brereton, C.Murphy, D.Prosser, A.Watson, A.Clues, I.Owens.
Referee: Mr. P. Cowell (Warrington)
Attendance: 77,605. Receipts: £17,434.

1948

Saturday 1st May 1948, at Wembley Stadium
Wigan 8, Bradford Northern 3.
Wigan: Tries: Hilton, Barton.
Goal: Ward.
Bradford: Try: Edwards.
WIGAN: M.Ryan; G.Ratcliffe, E.H.Ward, E.Ashcroft, J.Hilton; C.Mountford, T.Bradshaw; K.Gee, J.Egan, F.Barton, L.White, W.Blan, W.Hudson.
BRADFORD: W.Leake; E.Batten, D.Case, E.Ward, A.Edwards; W.T.H.Davies, D.Ward; F.Whitcombe, V.Darlison, H.Smith, T.Foster, B.Tyler, K.Traill.
Referee: Mr. G. S. Phillips (Widnes)
Attendance: 91,465. Receipts: £21,121.

1949

Saturday 7th May 1949, at Wembley Stadium
Bradford Northern 12, Halifax 0.
Bradford: Tries: Batten, Foster.
Goals: E.Ward (3).
BRADFORD: W.Leake; E.Batten, J.Kitching, E.Ward, A.Edwards; W.T.H.Davies, D.Ward; F.Whitcombe, V.Darlison, R.Greaces, T.Foster, B.Tyler, K.Traill.
HALIFAX: D.Chalkley; A.Daniels, P.J.Reid, G.Price, E.McDonald; G.Kenny, S.Keilty; M.J.Condon, A.Ackerley, J.W.Rothwell, D.Healy, J.Pansegrouw, F.Mawson.
Referee: Mr. G. S. Phillips (Widnes)
Attendance: 95,050. Receipts: £21,930.

Championship Finals

(Above)
Huddersfield captain Pat Devery receives the Championship trophy in 1949 from the RFL's President, the Earl of Derby, watched by Bill Fallowfield. On the right is Fartown's hooker Mel Meek.

(Above)
Alan Edwards - Salford's Welsh international who played as a guest for Dewsbury in war-time Championship Finals.

During the war Rugby League held Finals to decide the winners of the War Emergency League, before the fully fledged Northern Rugby League Championship Final (based on the top-four play-off) returned with great success in 1946. In the first season following the outbreak of the war in September 1939, a late decision was made to play a 'Championship Final' between the winners of the Lancashire and Yorkshire Leagues - which turned out to be Swinton and Bradford Northern - although no trophy or medals were presented. Victory for Bradford in this 1940 Final was the club's first major success since their reformation in 1907, and Northern repeated the feat by walloping Wigan in 1941.

Those war years saw clubs include numerous guest players in Championship Finals and none did that more successfully than Dewsbury who appeared in three consecutive Finals in 1942, '43 and '44. Under the managership of Eddie Waring, Dewsbury ran into controversy when their two-legged victory over Halifax in the 1943 Championship Final was declared 'null and void' on a technicality after Bradford Northern complained that Dewsbury had fielded an ineligible player (the Castleford forward Frank Smith) when they met in the Championship semi-final.

After the war, the Championship Final returned to Manchester City's Maine Road ground at the climax of the 1945-46 season, where Wigan made up for their disappointment of losing the Cup Final at Wembley by beating Huddersfield 13-4. Wigan, without four of their biggest stars on their way to Australia as members of the *Indomitables* touring team - Martin Ryan, Ted Ward, Joe Egan and Ken Gee - were captained by Welshman Eddie Watkins. An attendance of over 67,000 proved Maine Road's credentials as the best venue in the north capable of accommodating the crowds who wanted to attend the Championship Final which rapidly gained a reputation of providing a more entertaining game than the Wembley showpiece; although having to play the 1947 Final in late June - due to the fixture backlog caused by the winter freeze - saw the crowd drop by a whopping 27,000.

(Above) A newspaper illustration previewing the 1947 Championship Final - the cutting was headlined 'Wigan stars versus Dewsbury grit' - it was the stars who prevailed as Wigan won 13-4 at Maine Road.

War-time Emergency League Championship Finals

1940

Bradford beat Swinton 37-22 on aggregate.

First leg: Saturday 18th May 1940, at Station Road.
Swinton 13, Bradford Northern 21.
Attendance: 4,856. Receipts: £237.
Second leg: Saturday 25th May 1940, at Odsal Stadium.
Bradford Northern 16, Swinton 9.
Attendance: 11,271. Receipts: £570.

1941

Bradford beat Wigan 45-15 on aggregate.

First leg: Saturday 12th April 1941, at Centrak Park.
Wigan 6, Bradford Northern 17.
Attendance: 11,245. Receipts: £642,
Second leg: Monday 14th April 1941, at Odsal Stadium.
Bradford Northern 28, Wigan 9.
Attendance: 20,205.
Receipts: £1,148.

1942

Final: Saturday 18th April 1942, at Headingley, Leeds.
Dewsbury 13, Bradford Northern 0.
Attendance: 18,000.
Receipts: £1,121.

(Above) Dewsbury's Harry Royal played four Championship Finals in the 1940s.

1943

Dewsbury beat Halifax 33-16 on aggregate.

(But result declared 'null and void' after an enquiry)
First leg: Saturday 15th May 1943, at Crown Flatt.
Dewsbury 11, Halifax 3.
Attendance: 7,000. Receipts: £400.
Second leg: Saturday 22nd May 1943, at Thrum Hall.
Halifax 13, Dewsbury 22.
Attendance: 9,700. Receipts: £683.

1944

Wigan beat Dewsbury 25-14 on aggregate.

First leg: Saturday 13th May 1944, at Central Park.
Wigan 13, Dewsbury 9.
Attendance: 14,000. Receipts: £915.
Second leg: Saturday 20th May 1944, at Crown Flatt.
Dewsbury 5, Wigan 12.
Attendance: 9,000. Receipts: £680.

1945

Bradford beat Halifax 26-20 on aggregatre.

First leg: Saturday 19th May 1945, at Thrum Hall.
Halifax 9, Bradford Northern 2.
Attendance: 9,426. Receipts: £955.
Second leg: Monday 21st May 1945, at Odsal Stadium.
Bradford Northern 24, Halifax 11.
Attendance: 16,000. Receipts: £1,850.

(Top and right) Bradford Northern's Frank Whitcombe sees his tackle send Warrington's Jimmy Featherstone over his shoulder and into the turf in the 1948 Championship Final.

(Above) Wigan captain Joe Egan chaired by his team after winning the Championship Final of 1947.

(Left) Lord Derby on duty again as he presents the trophy to Warrington's captain Harold Palin after the 1948 Championship Final. The Wire had just defeated Bradford Northern 15-5 at Maine Road.

Wigan retained the title in that 1947 Final as they beat Dewsbury, this time without guest players, but Joe Egan's men failed to make it a hat-trick in 1948, despite finishing as league leaders, when they were beaten at Central Park by Bradford Northern in the top-four semi-final. Instead, it was second placed Warrington who came through to beat Bradford in the Final, thus winning the Championship for the first time in their history. Captained by loose-forward Harold 'Moggy' Palin, and guided by their astute manager Chris Brockbank, the Wire dominated Bradford to win 15-5 at Maine Road.

Warrington returned to contest the 1949 Championship Final with Huddersfield in a classic match which attracted a record crowd of 75,194. The men from Fartown had finished in third place, with Warrington top and Wigan second, but the star-studded outfit in claret and gold inflicted yet another home semi-final defeat on Wigan and edged ahead of Warrington 13-12 to be crowned champions. This was the ultimate triumph for this much admired Huddersfield side, which included the famous Australian trio Johnny Hunter, Lionel Cooper and captain Pat Devery, along with a cosmopolitan mix of Scots, Welshmen, Cumbrians and an Irishman.

NORTHERN RUGBY
CHAMPIONSHIP
FINAL
FOOTBALL LEAGUE

HUDDERSFIELD
v.
WARRINGTON
at
MAINE ROAD, MANCHESTER

SATURDAY, 14th MAY, 1949
Kick-off 3-0 p.m.

OFFICIAL PROGRAMME   SIXPENCE

(Above) Huddersfield, the Northern Rugby League Champions of the 1948-49 season, pictured behind the grandstand at Fartown before going out to play in front of the terraces packed with adoring supporters. The 'claret and golds' beat Warrington 13-12 in a thrilling Championship Final at Maine Road, Manchester.

1946

Saturday 18th May 1946, at Maine Road, Manchester.

Wigan 13, Huddersfield 4.

Wigan: Tries: Ashcroft (2), Cunliffe.
Goals: Nordgren (2).
Huddersfield: Goals: Bawden (2).
WIGAN: J.Cunliffe; B.Nordgren, G.Ratcliffe, E.Ashcroft, G.Jolley: R.Lowrey, T.Bradshaw; G.Banks, J.Blan, F.Barton, E.Watkins, H.Atkinson, W.Blan.
HUDDERSFIELD: W.Leake; J.Anderson, A.Fiddes, W.Davies, J.Bawden; T.L.Grahame, W.E.Morgan; K.Mallinson, H.Whitehead, J.Bradbury, J.Aspinall, L.Baxter, R.Robson.
Referee: Mr. A. S. Dobson (Pontefract).
Attendance: 67,136. Receipts: £8,386.

1947

Saturday 21st June 1947, at Maine Road, Manchester.

Wigan 13, Dewsbury 4.

Wigan: Tries: Nordgren, Lawrenson, Bradshaw.
Goals: Ward (2).
Dewsbury: Goals: Ledgard, Holt.
WIGAN: J.Cunliffe; B.Nordgren, E.Ward, E.Ashcroft, J.Lawrenson; C.Mountford, T.Bradshaw; K.Gee, J.Egan, G.Banks, F.Barton, W.Blan, J.Blan.
DEWSBURY: J.Ledgard; D.Armitage, G.Clark, K.Sacker, G.Withington; C.Gilbertson, H.Royal; H.Hammond, V.McKeating, B.Pearson, F.Cox, J.Holt, A.Street.
Referee: Mr. A. S. Dobson (Pontefract).
Attendance: 40,599. Receipts: £5,894.

1948

Saturday 8th May 1948, at Maine Road, Manchester.

Warrington 15, Bradford Northern 5.

Warrington: Tries: Bevan, Pimblett, Powell.
Goals: Palin (3).
Bradford N. Try: Case. Goal: E.Ward.
WARRINGTON: L.Jones; B.Bevan, B.Knowelden, A.Pimblett, S.Powell; J.Fleming, G.Helme; W.Derbyshire, D.Cotton, W.Riley, J.Featherstone, R.Ryan, H.Palin.
BRADFORD N.: G.Carmichael; E.Batten, D.Case, E.Ward, A.Edwards; W.T.H.Davies, D.Ward; F.Whitcombe, V.Darlison, H.Smith, T.Foster, B.Tyler, K.Traill.
Referee: Mr. A. S. Dobson (Pontefract).
Attendance: 69,143. Receipts: £9,791.

1949

Saturday 14th May 1949, at Maine Road, Manchester.

Huddersfield 13, Warrington 12.

Huddersfield: Tries: Devery, Cooper, Daly.
Goals: Devery (2).
Warrington: Tries: Jackson, Francis.
Goals: Bath (2), Palin.
HUDDERSFIELD: J.Hunter; J.Anderson, A.Ferguson, P.Devery, L.Cooper; R.Pepperell, W.Banks; M.Maiden, M.Meek, J.Daly, I.Owens, R.Nicholson, D.Valentine.
WARRINGTON: L.Jones; B.Bevan, A.Pimblett, W.Jackson, R.Francis; J.Fleming, G.Helme; W.Derbyshire, H.Fishwick, W.Riley, H.Bath, J.Featherstone, H.Palin.
Referee: Mr. M. Coates (Pudsey)
Attendance: 75,194. Receipts: £11,073.

Lancashire Cup Finals

(Above)
A very familiar sight in the 'forties - that of Wigan captain Joe Egan lifting the Lancashire Cup with a proud coach Jim Sullivan by his side This was after their 1949 win in the Final against Leigh.

(Above, right)
But Wigan didn't quite have a 100% record as Widnes beat them in the 1945 Final, in which Colin Hutton kicked two goals for the Chemics.

U nlike its Yorkshire counterpart, the Lancashire County Cup was unable to be maintained during World War Two, although the competition was played in the first season following the outbreak of hostilities culminating in a two-legged final between Swinton and Widnes played in April 1940. The Lions came through to win on aggregate after winning the first leg at Widnes 5-4 and the return at Station Road 16-11 after extra-time. At the end of normal time the Chemics were ahead 9-8, thus tying the aggregate score. Swinton were grateful for the goal-kicking of their, by then veteran, international second-row-forward Martin Hodgson who landed five successful shots in their second leg victory to win the Lancashire Cup.

When peace broke out in 1945 the competition was revived and, for the rest of the decade, it was dominated by Wigan. The cherry and whites appeared in every one of the five finals subsequently played in the 'forties, winning all but the first one. On that occasion, in October 1945, Widnes got the measure of Wigan at Wilderspool, beating them 7-3 and being guided by their experienced trio of Tommy McCue, Fred Higgins and Harry Millington. Thereafter, the red and white ribbons were a permanent fixture on the old county trophy and the sight of Joe Egan lifting it became very familiar.

Lancashire Cup Finals in the 'Forties

1945
Saturday 27th October 1945 at Wilderspool, Warrington.
Widnes 7, Wigan 3.
Widnes: Try: Reynolds. Goals: Hutton (2).
Wigan: Try: Toohey.
WIDNES: J.Bourke; M.Roberts, C.Hutton, A.Dagnall, A.Malone; C.Reynolds, T.McCue; A.Higgins, J.Hayes, H.McDowell, R.Roberts, F.Higgins, H.Millington.
WIGAN: M.Ryan; G.Ratcliffe, E.Ashcroft, E.Toohey, E.Ward; J.Fleming, T.Bradshaw; K.Gee, J.Egan, G.Banks, F.Barton, H.Atkinson, J.Blan.
Referee: Mr. R. Rawlinson (Rotherham).
Attendance: 28,184. Receipts: £2,604.

1946
Saturday 26th October 1946 at Station Road, Swinton.
Wigan 9, Belle Vue Rangers 3.
Wigan: Try: J.Blan. Goals: Lawrenson (3).
Belle Vue Rangers: Try: Manning.
WIGAN: M.Ryan; B.Nordgren, J.Lawrenson, E.Ashcroft, G.Ratcliffe; C.Mountford, T.Bradshaw; K.Gee, J.Egan, G.Banks, W.Blan, H.Atkinson, J.Blan.
BELLE VUE: A.Harris; T.Tolan, J.Waring, S.Powell, T.Barr; T.Kenny, W.Watkins; D.Thomas, G.Jones, A.Glendenning, E.Gwyther, W.Brown, R.Manning.
Referee: Mr. A. S. Dobson (Pontefract).
Attendance: 21,648. Receipts: £2,658.

(Above) The programme shows the team line-ups for the 1949 Lancashire Cup Final between Wigan and Leigh at Warrington.

(Above) Elwyn Gwyther and Doug Phillips, two Welsh international forwards who helped Belle Vue Rangers to the 1947 Lancashire Cup Final. The Manchester club played in two Finals in successive years.

The Wigan captain led his team in all four of their victorious Lancashire Cup Finals, the first against Belle Vue Rangers in 1946 as the Manchester side enjoyed a successful start to their first season after changing their name from Broughton Rangers. With a strong Welsh presence, Belle Vue were a good team, but couldn't quite manage to lower Wigan's colours in the Lancashire Cup. When Egan's men met Warrington in the 1948 Final a crowd of over 39,000 reflected the popularity of the county cup.

1947

Saturday 1st November 1947 at Wilderspool, Warrington.

Wigan 10, Belle Vue Rangers 7.

Wigan: Tries: Nordgren, Ratcliffe. Goals: Ward (2).
Belle Vue Rangers: Try: Flanagan. Goals: Thomas (2).
WIGAN: M.Ryan; B.Nordgren, E.Ward, G.Roughley, G.Ratcliffe; E.Ashcroft, T.Bradshaw; K.Gee, J.Egan, G.Banks, L.White, W.Blan, J.Blan
BELLE VUE: W.Ratchford; H.Pimblett, M.Tierney, S.McCormick, S.Jolley; R.Price, W.Watkins; D.Thomas, W.Flanagan, E.Gwyther, D.Phillips, J.Fearnley, R.Manning.
Referee: Mr. S. Adams (Hull).
Attendance: 23,110. Receipts: £3,043.

(Above) The Wigan team take an open top bus ride as they brought the Lancashire Cup home again in 1947 - beating Belle Vue at Wilderspool.

1948

Saturday 13th November 1948 at Station Road, Swinton.

Wigan 14, Warrington 8.

Wigan: Tries: Ratcliffe, Ward. Goals: Ward (4).
Warrington: Tries: Bevan, Johnson. Goal: Palin.
WIGAN: M.Ryan; G.Ratcliffe, E.Ward, E.Ashcroft, J.Lawrenson; C.Mountford, J.Alty; K.Gee, J.Egan, F.Barton, N.Silcock, W.Blan, W.Hudson.
WARRINGTON: L.Jones; B.Bevan, A. Pimblett, O.Peake, A.Johnson; J.Fleming, G.Helme; W.Derbyshire, D.Cotton, W.Riley, H.Bath, J.Featherstone, H.Palin.
Referee: Mr. S. Adams (Hull).
Attendance: 39,015. Receipts: £5,518.

1949

Saturday 29th October 1949 at Wilderspool, Warrington.

Wigan 20, Leigh 7.

Wigan: Tries: Nordgren (4), Hilton, W.Blan.
Goal: Gee.
Leigh: Try: Cleworth. Goals: Ledgard (2).
WIGAN: M.Ryan; J.Hilton, J.Cunliffe, E.Ashcroft, B.Nordgren; C.Mountford, T.Bradshaw; K.Gee, J.Egan, E.Slevin, F.Barton, W.Hudson, W.Blan.
LEIGH: J.Ledgard; J.Wood, E.Kerwick, N.Harris, A.Cleworth; J.Rowe, P.Riley; R.Edge, T.Stephens, R.Wheatley, C.Ryan, C.Pawsey, G.Burke.
Referee: Mr. G. S. Phillips (Widnes).
Attendance: 35,000. Receipts: £4,751.

Yorkshire Cup Finals

(*Above*)
Hull winger Tommy Glynn on the attack against Wakefield in the 1946 Yorkshire Cup Final at Leeds - won 10-0 by Trinity.

The Yorkshire Cup managed to maintain competition throughout the war years, with the familiar pattern of teams being boosted by 'guest' players going even further as numerous clubs from the west of the Pennines were invited to take part in the absence of their own Lancashire Cup - among these were such illustrious names as Wigan, Barrow, Oldham and St.Helens. The first war-time Yorkshire Cup Final in 1940 had a summer time feel as it was played on 22nd June, and it brought a first ever major trophy for Featherstone Rovers as they beat neighbours Wakefield Trinity at Odsal with Rovers loose-forward Bill Sherwood in inspirational form.

Dewsbury's war-time exploits of attracting some big name guest players were also seen in the Yorkshire Cup, and when they won the 1942 Final against Huddersfield, they had eight 'guests' in their side including internationals Barney Hudson, Alan Edwards and George Curran from Salford and Roy Francis from Barrow. Likewise, Keighley enjoyed a rare Cup Final appearance in 1943 boosted by five Warrington players in their ranks.

Bradford Northern's status as, arguably, the leading club in the game in the 1940s was illustrated by their successes in the Yorkshire Cup as they took the trophy back to Odal six times. With the familiar names of Ernest Ward and his brother Donald to the fore - along with international stars like Eric Batten, Alan Edwards, W.T.H. ('Billy') Davies, Frank Whitcombe and Trevor Foster - Northern were always the team to beat in Yorkshire. The 'dream' Yorkshire Cup Final came in 1949, when Bradford lined up against the talented and cosmopolitan Huddersfield side. That showdown attracted a crowd of 36,000 to Headingley, but it was one occasion when the claret and gold had to play second fiddle as Ernest Ward's men won 11-4.

War-time competition Yorkshire Cup Finals

1939-40
Saturday 22nd June 1940, at Odsal Stadium, Bradford.
Featherstone Rovers 12, Wakefield T. 9.
Attendance: 7,077. Receipts: £403.

1940-41
Saturday 5th April 1941, at Fartown, Huddersfield.
Bradford Northern 15, Dewsbury 5.
Attendance: 13,316. Receipts: £939.

1941-42
Saturday 6th December 1941, at Fartown, Huddersfield.
Bradford Northern 24, Halifax 0.
Attendance: 5,989. Receipts: £635.

1942-43
Dewsbury beat Huddersfield 7-2 on agg.
First leg: Saturday 28th November 1942.
Dewsbury 7, Huddersfield 0.
Attendance: 11,000. Receipts: £680.
Second leg: Saturday 5th December 1942.
Huddersfield 2, Dewsbury 0.
Attendance: 6,252. Receipts: £618.

1943-44
Bradford N. beat Keighley 10-7 on agg.
First leg: Saturday 27th November 1943.
Bradford Northern 5, Keighley 2.
Attendance: 10,251.
Receipts: £757.
Second leg: Saturday 6th December 1943.
Keighley 5, Bradford Northern 5.
Attendance: 8,993. Receipts: £694.

1944-45
Halifax beat Hunslet 14-3 on aggregate.
First leg: Saturday 2nd December 1944.
Hunslet 3, Halifax 12.
Attendance: 11,213. Receipts: £744.
Second leg: Saturday 9th December 1944.
Halifax 2, Hunslet 0.
Attendance: 9,800. Receipts: £745.

(*Above*)
Joe Flanagan, played for Keighley in the 1943 Final.

(Right) Wakefield scrum-half Herbert Goodfellow pictured in action. Trinity proved to be Bradford Northern's strongest rivals in the Yorkshire Cup after the return of peace-time competition in 1945. Wakefield played in three consecutive Finals in 1945, '46 and '47 - winning the latter two. Sharlston boy Goodfellow was one of Trinity's key players and starred in their triumph over Leeds following a replay in 1947, after missing the 1946 win over Hull.

Yorkshire Cup Finals in the 'Forties

1945
Saturday 3rd November 1945, at Thrum Hall, Halifax.
Bradford Northern 5, Wakefield Trinity 2.
Bradford N. Try: Whitcombe. Goal: Carmichael.
Wakefield Trinity: Goal: Stott.
BRADFORD N.: G.Carmichael; E.Batten, J.Kitching, E.Ward, W.Best; D.Bennett, D.Ward; L.Higson, V.Darlison, F.Whitcombe, L.Roberts, A.Marklew, W.Hutchinson.
WAKEFIELD T.: W.Teall; R.Copley, W.Stott, J.Jones, D.Baddeley; R.Rylance, H.Goodfellow; H.Wilkinson, L.Marston, J.Higgins, H.Murphy, F.Moore, L.Bratley.
Referee: Mr. G. S. Phillips (Widnes).
Attendance: 24,252. Receipts: £1,930.

1946
Saturday 2nd November 1946, at Headingley, Leeds.
Wakefield Trinity 10, Hull 0.
Wakefield Trinity.: Tries: Rylance, Fletcher.
Goals: Perry (2).
WAKEFIELD T.: W.Teall; J.Perry, J.Jones, J.Croston, D.Baddeley; R.Rylance, A.Fletcher; H.Wilkinson, L.Marson, J.Higgins, H.Exley, H,Murphy, L.Bratley.
HULL: F.Miller; T.Glynn, I.Watts, A.Sinclair, A.Bowers; E.Lawrence, T.A.Johnson; F.W.Shillito, H.Wilkinson, S.Jimmison, J.Tindall, A.Shakesby.
Referee: Mr. G. S. Phillips (Widnes).
Attendance: 29,000. Receipts: £3,720.

1947
Saturday 1st November 1947, at Fartown, Huddersfield.
Wakefield Trinity 7, Leeds 7.
Wakefield: Try: Goodfellow. Goals: Stott (2).
Leeds: Try: Williams. Goals: Whitehead (2).
WAKEFIELD TRINITY: W.Teall; J.Perry, W.Stott, D.Boocker, R.Jenkinson; A.Fletcher, H.Goodfellow; H.Wilkinson, L.Marson, J.Higgins, H.Murphy, J.Booth, L.Bratley.
LEEDS: J.Kelly; D.Warrior, H.E.Cook, G.Price, E.Whitehead; R.Williams, D.Jenkins; D.Prosser, C.Carter, R.Wheatley, A.Clues, J.Flanagan, I.Owens.
Referee: Mr. G. S. Phillips (Widnes).
Attendance: 24,334. Receipts: £3,463.

1947 REPLAY
Wednesday 5th November 1947, at Odsal Stadium, B'fd.
Wakefield Trinity 8, Leeds 7.
Wakefield: Tries: Wilkinson, Bratley.
Goal: Perry.
Leeds: Try: Flanagan.
Goals: Cook, Whitehead.
WAKEFIELD TRINITY: Same team except R.Rylance replaced W.Stott in the threequarter line.
LEEDS: Same team except C.Brereton replaced R.Wheatley at blind-side prop.
Referee: Mr. G. S. Phillips (Widnes).
Attendance: 32,500. Receipts: £3,258.

1948
Saturday 30th October 1948, at Headingley, Leeds.
Bradford Northern 18, Castleford 9.
Bradford N.: Tries: Edwards (2), Leake, Foster.
Goals: Edwards (3).
Castleford: Try: Foreman.
Goals: Langfield, Foreman, Staines.
BRADFORD N.: G.Carmichael; E.Batten, W.Leake, E.Ward, A.Edwards; W.T.H.Davies, D.Ward; F.Whitcombe, V.Darlison, R.Greaves, T.Foster, B.Tyler, K.Traill.
CASTLEFORD: R.Lewis; A.Bartsow, L.Skidmore, N.Guest, R.Lloyd; A.Fisher, G.Langfield; D.L.Harris, J.Jones, J.Crossley, D.Foreman, C.Staines, F.Mugglestone.
Referee: Mr. G. S. Phillips (Widnes).
Attendance: 31,393. Receipts: £5,053.

1949
Saturday 29th October 1949, at Headingley, Leeds.
Bradford Northern 11, Huddersfield 4.
Bradford N.: Try: Davies. Goals: E.Ward (4).
Huddersfield: Goals: Bawden (2).
BRADFORD N.: W.Leake; E.Batten, E.Ward, J.Kitching, E.Walters; W.T.H.Davies, D.Ward; E.Day, V.Darlison, R.Greaves, B.Tyler, T.Foster, K.Traill.
HUDDERSFIELD: E.Swallow; G.Wilson, J.Bawden, P.Devery, L.Cooper; R.Pepperell, W.Banks; J.Maiden, M.Meek, J.Daly, I.Owens, R.Nicholson, D.Valentine.
Referee: Mr. W. Hemmings (Halifax).
Attendance: 36,000. Receipts: £6,365.

Birth of Cumberland clubs

WORKINGTON TOWN R.F.L. CLUB

Back Row:
Cavanagh, Acherley, Holding, Shearman, Miller, Hayton (J.).
Middle Row:
Rodgers, Carr, Hodgson, Jackson, Ireing.
Front Row:
Jepson, Pepperell.

PHOTOGRAPH BY DR. T. T. GRAHAM, WORKINGTON

(Above)
Gus Risman in training as leader of Workington Town at Borough Park

Rugby League spread its wings in the 1940s with the introduction of two new senior clubs from Cumberland. It remains one of the most unequivocal examples of the game setting up new professional clubs due entirely to public demand. West Cumberland had long been an area that was a hot bed of Rugby League, with well established amateur clubs and big crowds regularly drawn to watch home fixtures of the County team - indeed international matches had been staged there. The biggest question was just why it had taken so long to set up a professional club in Cumberland which, since the very birth of the Northern Union, had built a minor industry out of the exportation of talented rugby players to the clubs of Lancashire and Yorkshire.

Workington Town were the first of the two Cumbrian clubs, they entered the Northern Rugby League in the first post-war season of 1945-46, and enjoyed an impressive opening fixture when they defeated the famous name of Broughton Rangers 27-5 on 25th August 1945. Sharing Borough Park with the local soccer club, Town attracted average attendances of just over 8,000 in their first season when their young side played attractive open football but eventually had to bow to more experienced opposition and finished in 19th position in the league (out of 27 teams). Workington's master stroke was their recruitment of Gus Risman from Salford as player-coach as they began their second season - although they had to wait several weeks into the campaign for Gus to return from his epic journey as captain of the 1946 *Indomitables*. The presence of Risman acted like a pied-piper for the Cumbrian public and big crowds, regularly over five figures, began to flock to Borough Park which quickly made Town one of the most vibrant clubs in the game.

In their second season Workington rose to an 11th place finish and their remarkable progression continued as their third season, 1947-48, saw them achieve fifth place in the league, just one spot away from a coveted top-four play-off position. Those wonderful times at Borough Park continued with the Town Supporters' Club enrolling over 8,000 members as the incomparable 'Gus' went on to achieve his master plan by leading Workington to both the Championship and Challenge Cup within seven years of the club's birth.

Workington's success only encouraged the launch of a second professional club eight miles down the Cumbrian coast at Whitehaven in 1948. Closely tied to the local mining industry, Whitehaven's acceptance into the Northern Rugby League was not without struggle as they were only admitted by 14 votes to 11 by the game's governing Council. One club not in favour of a new club at Whitehaven were their near neighbours Workington, who felt all local support and resources should be channelled into one club in the area rather than split between two, but Town quickly changed their tune when they counted the gate receipts for their home derby matches as, in Whitehaven's first season, over 16,000 were at Borough Park, rising to over 19,000 in their second campaign.

Whitehaven played their first match in the Northern Rugby League on 21st August 1948, and celebrated with a 5-nil victory over Hull. Unfortunately torrential rain at their largely uncovered ground badly hit expectations of a five figure crowd, but it was still estimated that as many as 9,000 souls had braved the elements. Whitehaven had appointed Gus Risman's fellow *Indomitable* Jack Kitching as their inaugral player-coach in the hope that he could have the same mesmeric effect as Gus. But their hopes for Kitching did not materialise and he left just half way through the first season in which the so called 'Babes' finished just three rungs from the bottom of the league in 27th place. Steady improvement came in their second campaign, 1949-50, under player-coach Ned Hodgson, the experienced prop-forward who had previously served the Workington club in its earliest days. Another early link, of what was to become many, between the two Cumbrian clubs was the role played by Mr. Tom Mageen as chairman of both in their debut seasons.

The game in France

Nowhere in the world was the game involved in more drama during the 'forties than in France. With the nation under German occupation from early in the war it was only to be expected that things would be difficult for the continuation of any sport, but nobody could have foreseen the bitter blow inflicted exclusively on Rugby League. It was banned - refused permission to exist - by order of the wartime Vichy government. As early as August 1940 declarations had been made forbidding the organisation of Rugby League matches, with the order that all players and clubs should, forthwith, play Rugby Union instead. But the final *coup de grace* - the dagger in the heart of the young and vibrant Rugby League movement - came on 19th December 1941 when an official decree, signed by Marshal Petain, Head of the French State, dissolved the French Rugby League, having refused authorisation for it to exist anymore. And in the same decree it was instructed that all property of the dissolved organisation be transferred in its entirety to the National Sports Committee. Rugby League in France was dead! And, at the same time, the considerable assets the French League had built up in its incredibly successful first five years, from 1934 to 1939, had been taken from it.

Historians looking in from the outside might wonder just why this one sport, and no other, was deemed so undesirable by the Vichy government that they had to kill it. Was there something about it their masters in Nazi Germany particularly hated or feared? Perhaps the fact that the French Rugby League had enjoyed very close links with the British in the years immediately before the war? But, in truth, the reason for the cruel fate inflicted upon Rugby League had nothing to do with the Nazis, it was purely and simply an act of sabotage committed by French Rugby Union men, desperate for revenge on this 'new rugby' which had enjoyed such popularity in its short life in France that it had built a seemingly unstoppable momentum. Among the several Rugby Union men in office with the Vichy government, Colonel Joseph Pascot was the Director of Sports. Pascot was a former Union international player and all evidence pointed to him as the man who deliberately killed Rugby League.

As the fortunes of the war began to swing in favour of the Allies, the first moves began among enthusiasts in France to try and revive Rugby League. An initial meeting was held at the Hotel Regina in Toulouse on 16th September 1944 at which a 24-year-old Paul Barriere was an interested observer, invited to attend by the wily old Perpignan official Marcel Laborde. Barriere had been a Resistance leader and, as such, was no lover of the Vichy goverment - Laborde knew that the young Barriere was the man to carry the fight to have Rugby League resurrected, but it proved to be a long struggle against the corridors of power in

(Above)
Robert Caillou of Bayonne, an inspiring captain for France in the years immediately after World War Two.

(Above)
Puig-Aubert and Paul Dejean in London for France's match at Wembley in 1949 - and yes, 'Popaul' is wearing his slippers!

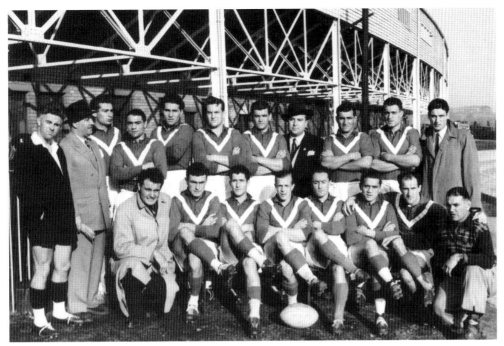

Paris before official approval was given for the game to be recognised as an independent sport - and even then it came with the condition that it could not use the word 'rugby' (which was reserved for Rugby Union only) so instead it had to adopt the name of *Jeu a X111* - which translated means 'game of thirteen'. Barriere was elected President of the newly named *Federation Francaise de Jeu a X111* at their conference at Bayonne in July 1947, and became a charismatic figure as French Rugby League enjoyed its golden era in the decade immediately after World War Two.

(Above)
Paul Dejean captain of the Catalans as they became the first team to win the Lord Derby Cup after the French Rugby League's post-war revival in 1945.

The game enjoyed a symbollic revenge on its disgraced Rugby Union assassins as hordes of players flocked to play the 'new rugby' and it was ironic that over half of the champion 1944 Perpignan Rugby Union side (Colonel Pascot's team) switched to the League game which had been denied them during the war years, among them some who became French Rugby League's biggest stars: Puig-Aubert, Jo Crespo, Gaston Comes, Paul Dejean and Elie Brousse. Big crowds flocked to watch a vibrant French championship, which included a new stellar club formed in the city of Marseille in 1946 and financed by wealthy local businessmen including the celebrated Paul Ricard. Roanne, backed by Claude Devernois, continued where they had left off before the war, and a new power emerged at Carcassonne who achieved the incredible record of playing in every one of the ten major finals staged in the 'forties. With Puig-Aubert their biggest attraction, Carcassonne won a double in 1946, a feat repeated by Marseille (starring Jean Dop) in 1949. The *X111 Catalan* were the first Cup winners after the war in 1945 captained by Paul Dejean - the man who also skippered the *Catalans de France* to a famous 20-5 win over the Australian tourists in Perpignan on Christmas Day 1948. It was just one of many great moments for French Rugby League in the 'forties although the game suffered a major loss with the sudden death of its founder, Jean Galia, in January 1949 at the premature age of 44.

CHAMPIONSHIP FINALS
1945 - Carcassonne beat Toulouse, 13-12. (at Perpignan)
1946 - Carcassonne beat Toulouse, 12-0. (at Lyon)
1947 - Roanne beat Carcassonne, 19-0. (at Lyon)
1948 - Roanne beat Carcassonne, 3-2. (at Marseille)
1949 - Marseille beat Carcassonne, 12-5. (at Carcassonne)

COUPE de FRANCE FINALS
1945 - X111 Catalan beat Carcassonne, 27-18. (at Paris)
1946 - Carcassonne beat X111 Catalan, 27-7. (at Toulouse)
1947 - Carcassonne beat Avignon, 24-5. (at Marseille)
1948 - Marseille beat Carcassonne, 5-4. (at Toulouse)
1949 - Marseille beat Carcassonne, 12-9. (at Marseille)

The County Championship

Cumberland, who had enjoyed such success in the 1930s, struggled behind their Yorkshire and Lancashire counterparts in trying to revive their county team in the first season after the war - and a hastily cobbled together side was thrashed at Leeds by the white rose in 1945. Yet, two years later when they returned to the same venue, the Cumbrians were back to 'normal' and inflicted a 15-7 defeat on Yorkshire. The following season, in 1948-49, Cumberland were County Champions, and throughout the 'forties they were the only team to draw a 10,000-plus crowd to every one of their home fixtures in the County Championship. Lancashire, with a strong Wigan and Warrington contingent, were the most successful county in the 'forties.

(Above, left)
The Cumberland side hastily put together for their first post-war fixture at Headingley on 31 October 1945.
(Above, right)
Yorkshire, captained by Jimmy Ledgard, before playing Lancashire in 1949.

County Championship results in the 'Forties

1945-46
Wednesday 31 October 1945, at Headingley, Leeds.
Yorkshire 45, Cumberland 3. *Att.: 3,500.*
Saturday 10 November 1945, at Station Road, Swinton.
Lancashire 17, Yorkshire 16. *Att.: 11,059.*
Saturday 26 January 1946, at Borough Park, Workington.
Cumberland 3, Lancashire 18. *Att.: 10,026.*
County Champions: Lancashire.

1946-47
Thursday 26 September 1946, at Borough Park, Workington.
Cumberland 9, Yorkshire 11. *Att.: 11,300.*
Saturday 9 November 1946, at Parkside, Hunslet.
Yorkshire 13, Lancashire 10. *Att.: 5,000.*
Saturday 4th January 1947, at Craven Park, Barrow.
Lancashire 0, Cumberland 0. *Att.: 8,148.*
County Champions: Yorkshire.

1947-48
Wednesday 22 October 1947, at Headingley, Leeds.
Yorkshire 7, Cumberland 15. *Att.: 3,500.*
Wednesday 12 November 1947, at Central Park, Wigan.
Lancashire 22, Yorkshire 10. *Att.: 6,270.*
Saturday 15 May 1948, at Borough Park, Workington.
Cumberland 13, Lancashire 20. *Att.: 12,000.*
County Champions: Lancashire.

1948-49
Wednesday 6 April 1949, at Borough Park, Workington.
Cumberland 14, Yorkshire 0. *Att.: 12,000.*
Wednesday 20 April 1949, at The Willows, Salford.
Lancashire 9, Cumberland 15.
Att.: 6,000.
Tuesday 3 May 1949, at Thrum Hall, Halifax.
Yorkshire 3, Lancashire 12.
Att.: 7,000.
County Champions: Cumberland.

1949-50
Monday 26 September 1949, at the Boulevard, Hull.
Yorkshire 21, Cumberland 8. *Att.: 9,325.*
Wednesday 5 October 1949, at Wilderspool, Warrington.
Lancashire 22, Yorkshire 13. *Att.: 15,000.*
Wednesday 12 October 1949, at Borough Park, Workington.
Cumberland 22, Lancashire 11. *Att.: 10,000.*
Championship undecided - all teams two points each.

(Above) Billy Ivison tackled by Eric Batten in Cumberland's win over Yorkshire in 1949.